Destroying the Lies

Combating Satan with Biblical Truth

Destroying the Lies

For information contact:
http://www.bridgethegapministry.com

Cover design and illustration by Sarah Chapman
Photography by Kira Cupp at Nothing Rhymes with Orange, LLC
Book design by Billie Jewel Sexton
Edited by Sallie Vandagrift
ISBN: 978-0-578-846446
First Edition: November 2021

Dedication

This book is dedicated to my husband, Sean, whose support constantly fuels my dreams for this ministry. And to my children, may you always know your worth in God.

Acknowledgements

Thank you to my mother, Donna Brumfield, for your steadfast unconditional love. Thank you to my stepfather, Larry, for believing and encouraging my goals. Thank you to my best friend, Sarah Chapman, for always providing a safe space to express myself and for using your God-given artistic talent to help bring my passions to life. I love you all!

Contents

"Stay alert! Watch out for your great enemy, the devil. He prowls around like a roaring lion, looking for someone to devour."

– 1 Peter 5:8

Preface

I remember very clearly walking into the dimly lit auditorium, worship music playing, passing all of the seemingly perfect people with their hands held high in praise. All the while, running through my mind on a loop was: *You will never be as good as them, as deserving as them, as pure as them. They are worth so much more than you.* It was in my head and it was crushing my heart, but I never dared speak it out loud. I nodded my head anytime the pastor spoke about how we were all children of God, but every time my mind would say *except for you.* You see, I was always the exception. God forgave the sins of other believers, he gave grace in their failures, he poured blessings over and guided the path of everyone—except me. This was because I was carrying a huge secret, one so big that I felt if anyone found out the ground under me would collapse and I would be dragged to hell. A secret that I desperately tried to push out of my mind and forget but that ultimately left me filled with bitterness and rage. The weight of carrying around this darkness caused me to cut myself in attempts to gain control of the pain and made me put walls between myself and everyone I came in contact with.

What was my secret? I was sexually abused, and in my mind I was constantly trying to overcome the big neon sign across my forehead that read "used." I tried for many years to "handle it" myself, to get past it, forget it, pretend it did not happen. But it was more than I could take on myself. After fighting it for far too long, I eventually sought out counseling at the local sexual assault center. For six months I sat in my weekly session trying to convince my therapist I was only there to entertain her with stories of my many hobbies and vent about work. For six months I gave no hint or mention of any abuse, and thankfully for six months my therapist patiently waited for me to trust her. When I finally opened up, it was terrifying. As soon as the words left my mouth, I wanted to shove them back in. I want to say a weight was instantly lifted, but that is not the truth. The truth is that it was hard. There were many times I felt like I was sinking, but the difference now was that I was not alone. I had my therapist, I joined a support group, and eventually opened up to friends and family. While all of this helped it did not heal my wounds. It was not until I began to biblically fight my battles and thoughts with God's truth that I gained my present and my future.

There were a thousand little reasons I kept my secret, but the three main things that kept me from reaching out were shame, fear, and anger. I was so angry, not just at my abuser, but at God. And as a Christian, I did not know how to stand up and say, "I feel like God abandoned me, a God that loves me wouldn't let this happen, I am so furious with God!" So, I did not. I shut down and just faked my way through church, as so many of us do. The truth is that we may be afraid to ask, but God does not fear our questions. He is not dodging topics or crossing his fingers hoping that we will not corner him about unanswered prayers. Furthermore, there are many biblical examples of people asking God tough questions. Read through Psalms or Job in your Bible and you will see multiple instances where people cry out to God, asking why.

Unfortunately, there are many things that we will not have answers to on this side of heaven. What I can tell you is that God loves you. He sees and knows every part of you, every part. And still, he loves you. If you have been abused, I get it. I know that you want to pull back and hide, but I am telling you if you will just surrender it all to God, he will make beauty from the ashes. He knows what was done to you and he knows what you have done to cope, what you have done out of hurt, anger, fear; and still, he loves you.

Romans 8:38–39 says, "For I am convinced that neither death, nor life, nor angels, nor principalities, nor things present, nor things to come, nor powers, nor height, nor depth, nor any other created thing will be able to separate us from the love of God, which is in Christ Jesus our Lord." Did you catch that? There is literally nothing, nothing you can do that will keep God from loving you. Nothing in your past, nothing in your present, and nothing in your future that will separate you from the love of our God! You can be mad, you may never understand the "why?" but please believe me when I say that laying that pain at the feet of Jesus can bring you a peace that surpasses understanding, and God will pull from your brokenness and give you a purpose that turns all things to good.

Blessing

I pray that as you begin reading about the lies Satan has used to attack you, your heart will be opened to learning and accepting the truth about your identity and value. I pray that all barriers, including anger, bitterness, judgment, and hurt, crumble and that every chain the devil has on you will be released. I declare in Jesus's name that nothing in this book will trigger you or cause you to stumble, but with every word you will grow closer to knowing and loving both yourself and God our Father. I pray that any shame or fear connected with reaching out for further help will be vanquished. I pray that this book will bring you peace and comfort, and will wrap you in love. Above all, I pray that by deconstructing these lies you'll be able to lay your burdens at the feet of Jesus so that he may heal you.

Helmet of Salvation

GOD

Every one of us has an opinion about God that is shaped by our environment and life experience. Maybe you are saved or an atheist, grew up in church, only attended on holidays, or have never stepped foot in a chapel, or perhaps your family practices a non-Christian religion. Your personal and unique upbringing plays a huge factor in how you see God. God, however, does not change according to our perspectives. God is who he is, unchanging and constant all the time.

The misinformation, myths, and flat-out lies surrounding who God is are too numerous to count. Much like the game of telephone, the truth of God often gets watered down or twisted when passed through culture. If you want to know who God truly is—his mind, his heart, his character—I highly suggest you stop listening to the world and go to the source: the Bible.

There is a wonderful quote by Charles Spurgeon that says, "Discernment is not knowing the difference between right and wrong. It is knowing the difference between right and almost right." You will meet many wonderful people in your life who have the best hopes and intentions of steering you in the direction of Christ. You will also meet many hurt and broken people who will feed you lies about God that they have bought into. It is up to you to do the fact-checking.

The following chapter lists seven lies about God that I have found to be the most prevalent in my research. I encourage you to find, highlight, and make notes surrounding the Bible verses listed. I also encourage you to read the passages these verses belong to. In order to have a true relationship with someone, you must know them. God is no different, you will get to know him, love him, and understand his deep love for you by reading his word.

If you do not own a Bible most churches and ministries give free Bibles gladly.

LIE:
God wants to control me.

TRUTH:
God wants to guide you so that you may walk in true freedom, peace, and joy.

"We can make our own plans, but the LORD gives the right answer."
– *Proverbs 16:1*

"We can make our plans, but the LORD determines our steps."
– *Proverbs 16:9*

"The LORD says, "I will guide you along the best pathway for your life.
I will advise you and watch over you."
– *Psalm 32:8*

God does not want to control you, he wants the best for you and above all, he wants your love. Though God is sovereign and capable of complete control of everything, he chose to give us free will. He did this because true love and faith are not nurtured from control but from the choice to believe, seek, and give ourselves to the Lord freely. Though our best possible lives are lived walking in line with God, he does not force us to do so. His caring heart in giving us a choice is revealed in Galatians 5:13 where we are told "For you have been called to live in freedom, my brothers and sisters. But do not use your freedom to satisfy your sinful nature. Instead, use your freedom to serve one another in love." This does not mean that God watches our lives as a spectator only, never intervening. God creates circumstances according to his divine plan and gives us constant opportunities to choose his path. First Corinthians 10:13 explains that "the temptations in your life are no different from what others experience. And God is faithful. He will not allow the temptation to be more than you can stand. When you are tempted, He will show you a way out so that you can endure" (NASB). Our freedom of choice is a gift from God so that we may experience his complete love. He opens doors, lays out paths, and constructs opportunities, but the choice within those circumstances is ours.

Encouragement

Being controlled or manipulated is a horrible feeling and wanting to avoid going through that experience again is completely understandable. But we cannot allow the pain of our past to dictate how we navigate our future. By mislabeling God as a controlling father, you are missing out on all of the opportunities and blessings he has for you.

Self-Study

How did this lie start? *Was it told to you or did you tell it to yourself? Was there a specific moment you started to believe this lie?*

____

____

____

____

____

____

____

____

Is there someone in your life *(past or present)* **who has tried to control you? How did it make you feel?**

____

____

____

____

How has this lie affected you? *Has this lie led to certain choices? Has this lie held you back from opportunities or joy?*

How would your life change if you believed the truth instead of this lie?

In the following columns add to the list of differences between loving guidance and control so that you may better differentiate between the two.

GUIDANCE	CONTROL
choices	*manipulation*
empowerment	*guilt*
comfort	*fear*

Pick a memory verse to repeat to yourself whenever this lie pops into your head and write it here.

LIE:
God only cares about Christians.

TRUTH:
God made and loves everyone, but we must choose to give our hearts to Jesus in order to have an intimate relationship with him.

"The second is equally important: 'Love your neighbor as yourself.' No other commandment is greater than these."
– *Mark 12:31*

"But God showed his great love for us by sending Christ to die for us while we were still sinners."
– *Romans 5:8*

God longs for a relationship with you, me, and every soul he created. We are instructed numerous times in the Bible of the importance of loving others, all others. This world has a bad habit of convincing us that we must hate or toss aside anyone that does not agree with or live like us. However, much of Jesus's life was spent purposely surrounded by sinners. Not because he agreed with them, not because he lowered or compromised standards, but because he cared about and loved them. This did not sit well with many, in fact Luke 15:2 tells us that "this made the Pharisees and teachers of religious law complain that he was associating with such sinful people—even eating with them!" But Jesus made his intentions clear in Luke 5:32, "I have come to call not those who think they are righteous, but those who know they are sinners and need to repent."

In both Matthew 18:12 and Luke 15:4, Jesus tells the parable of the lost sheep, where he compares God's love for us to that of a shepherd. In the parable, Jesus asks what shepherd having a hundred sheep would not leave the ninety-nine in the pasture to go after the one that is lost? In this, God is the shepherd, and the lost sheep represents anyone who does not know God or has turned away from him. It is true that God loves those who love him (Proverbs 8:17), but God's heart breaks for those who do not know him. He is seeking out the lost. Ezekiel 34:11 says, "For this is what the Sovereign Lord says: I myself will search and find my sheep." You do not seek that which you do not care for. God seeking the lost sheep is an expression of love. God cares about you. No matter how far you have run, how deep you have fallen, or how badly you feel you've messed up, God is seeking you out with open arms.

Encouragement

If you are struggling with believing God cares for you, I urge you to read Luke 15:11–32, the parable of the lost son. This parable tells us of a son that has left his family, squandered away his inheritance, and fears the disappointment and judgment of his father so much that he believes he will have to beg his father just to let him live as a servant in his home.

> "But while he (the son) was still a long way off, his father saw him and was filled with compassion for him; he ran to his son, threw his arms around him and kissed him. The son said to him, 'Father, I have sinned against heaven and against you. I am no longer worthy to be called your son.' But the father said to his servants, 'Quick! Bring the best robe and put it on him. Put a ring on his finger and sandals on his feet. Bring the fattened calf and kill it. Let's have a feast and celebrate. For this son of mine was dead and is alive again; he was lost and is found.' So they began to celebrate" (Luke 15:20–24).

God is willing and waiting to celebrate you just as this father did for his son!

Self-Study

How did this lie start? *Was it told to you or did you tell it to yourself? Was there a specific moment you started to believe this lie?*

____

____

How has this lie affected you? *Has this lie led to certain choices? Has this lie held you back from opportunities or joy?*

How would your life change if you believed the truth instead of this lie?

Pick a memory verse to repeat to yourself whenever this lie pops into your head and write it here.

LIE:
God does not want to bless me.

TRUTH:
God wants to bless you abundantly.

"And this same God who takes care of me will supply all your needs from his glorious riches, which have been given to us in Christ Jesus."
– Philippians 4:19

"And God will generously provide all you need. Then you will always have everything you need and plenty left over to share with others."
– 2 Corinthians 9:8

God's love for us is so pure, full, and deep that we will never truly understand its capacity until we meet him in heaven. It is that all-encompassing love for us that makes him want to bless us beyond our wildest imaginations. Often, we only recognize God's blessings when we have specifically asked for the blessings we have received. However, the vast majority of blessings are ones that we did not ask for or even notice. The blessing of waking up, the blessing of food, work, education, time. Sometimes things that appear to be failures turn out to be a blessing in the long run. Our perspective does not dictate whether we are being blessed, God's blessing are there even if we choose not to acknowledge them.

Certain blessings, though, require steps of faith and belief. Many of us keep quiet about our questions, struggles, and doubts, but our thoughts do not surprise God. If you are struggling with doubt, talk to God about it! Mark 9 tells of a father asking Jesus to cast out a demon in his son *if* he can. Now, I do not know about you, but when I first read that my heart jumped into my throat. I mean, did this man really just look into the eyes of the God of the universe and challenge him with *if you can*?! I fully expected the following verses to be about the wrath of God. Thankfully, though, Jesus saw beyond what you and I do and into the heart of the broken father standing before him who was both hopeful and struggling with very real doubt. In Mark 9:23–24, Jesus responds by asking, "What do you mean, 'If I can'?" Before the father could answer, Jesus continued, saying "Anything is possible if a person believes." The father instantly cried out, "I do believe, but help me overcome my unbelief!" It is possible to believe while also having doubt. If doubts are holding you back, cry out to God to break through chains and open your heart fully. He will help you!

Encouragement

I want to challenge you to get a journal or create a note on your phone to start recording each blessing from God. Do not just wait to capture the "big" stuff. Write down each blessing, no matter how small it may seem. It is amazing how many blessings you will find when you start purposefully seeking them.

Self-Study

How did this lie start? *Was it told to you or did you tell it to yourself? Was there a specific moment you started to believe this lie?*

____

____

____

____

____

____

____

____

How has this lie affected you? *Has this lie led to certain choices? Has this lie held you back from opportunities or joy?*

____

How would your life change if you believed the truth instead of this lie?

Pick a memory verse to repeat to yourself whenever this lie pops into your head and write it here.

LIE:
God does not want my brokenness.

TRUTH:
God wants every part of us, including our brokenness.

"The LORD is close to the brokenhearted; he rescues those whose spirits are crushed."
– *Psalm 34:18*

"Each time he said, 'My grace is all you need. My power works best in weakness.' So now I am glad to boast about my weaknesses, so that the power of Christ can work through me."
– *2 Corinthians 12:9*

God wants you to lay it all at his feet: your anger, shame, loneliness, loss, fear, and brokenness. He is the master of finding beauty in ashes and he can transform your hurt if you allow him to.

> For God, who said, "Let there be light in the darkness," has made this light shine in our hearts so we could know the glory of God that is seen in the face of Jesus Christ. We now have this light shining in our hearts, but we ourselves are like fragile clay jars containing this great treasure. This makes it clear that our great power is from God, not from ourselves. We are pressed on every side by troubles, but we are not crushed. We are perplexed, but not driven to despair. We are hunted down, but never abandoned by God. We get knocked down, but we are not destroyed (2 Corinthians 4:6–9).

Our brokenness displays our weakness and in that we see God's redemptive strength. Romans 8:28 tells us that God causes all things to work together for good. Yep, all things! Even your messy life, your past, your trauma, your mistakes; he can use it all! Do not just take my word for it, look to the Bible. Research literally anyone in the Bible and you will find that they, just like us, were humans with a whole lot of mess. David had an affair, Paul and Moses were murderers, Hosea's wife Gomer was a prostitute, yet God used them all! Time after time, we see the people of the Bible questioning their capabilities, feeling unworthy in their given path because of the people they were, and the things they have done. But God does not look at our past in blessing our future. Wherever you are today, God wants you.

Encouragement

Not only can God restore you, but he can also help you be a light to others who are struggling. Redemption is beautiful! To have your life completely transformed by the love of God is an astounding thing. There is power in your past and in your brokenness. Do not toss away or take lightly your strength of survival, your label of an over-comer, and your ability to speak life into others who are hurting!

Self-Study

How did this lie start? *Was it told to you or did you tell it to yourself? Was there a specific moment you started to believe this lie?*

How has this lie affected you? *Has this lie led to certain choices? Has this lie held you back from opportunities or joy?*

How would your life change if you believed the truth instead of this lie?

What are some ways you could use your brokenness to relate, connect, and help others?

Pick a memory verse to repeat to yourself whenever this lie pops into your head and write it here.

LIE:
God is angry at me.

TRUTH:
God gets angry at sin, but still loves sinful people.

"The LORD is merciful and compassionate, slow to get angry and filled with unfailing love."
– *Psalm 145:8*

"Love your enemies! Do good to them. Lend to them without expecting to be repaid. Then your reward from heaven will be very great, and you will truly be acting as children of the Most High, for he is kind to those who are unthankful and wicked. You must be compassionate, just as your Father is compassionate."
– *Luke 6:35–36*

When you repent God forgives your sins through Jesus's blood. Nowhere in the Bible does it say you must repent four hundred times for the sin you committed at twenty years old and then God will forgive you. Nowhere in the Bible does it say you are to repent of your sin but still carry the weight and shame of it for the rest of your life. Nor does it say God will only forgive you if you are perfect from here on out and never sin again. What the Bible does say is: "Now repent of your sins and turn to God, so that your sins may be wiped away" (Acts 3:19).

It is true that God hates sin and when we sin it makes him angry. However, somewhere along the way we have forgotten that you can be angry at someone while still loving them. Sin breaks God's heart and separates us from him but we have the power through repentance to walk in a close relationship with God. God is not avoiding you or holding back from you out of anger. If you feel separated from God, it is of your own choosing. I do not say that in trying to place blame, but to express that God deeply desires to be close to you. The devil wants you to believe that God is so angry at you that he could never possibly forgive you let alone love you. This is where the importance of fact checking comes in because the Bible tells us the truth:

that God loves you so much that he sent his son to die on a cross so that our sins could be covered. If you are not a believer, I am so thankful that you are reading this, that you are seeking truth and I encourage you to keep learning about how much Jesus loves you. If you are a believer take comfort in the fact that Jesus has paid for it all. Hebrews 9:14 reminds us to "think how much more the blood of Christ will purify our consciences from sinful deeds so that we can worship the living God. For by the power of the eternal Spirit, Christ offered himself to God as a perfect sacrifice for our sins."

Encouragement

God did not go through watching his son die on a cross so that he could hold on to anger or hang guilt or shame over your head. God endured the pain of Jesus dying because sin has a cost and must be paid in order for us to have a relationship with and experience the love of God. If you are feeling guilt or shame, know that those are tools of the devil, not of God. The devil uses guilt: feelings of deserving blame for offenses real or imagined (Merriam-Webster Dictionary). God uses conviction: the act of convincing a person of error, or of compelling the admission of a truth (Merriam-Webster Dictionary). God knew every sin you would commit before you were even born, your sins do not surprise him. Yes, God may get angry with our actions, but that does not take away from his love for us.

Self-Study

How did this lie start? *Was it told to you or did you tell it to yourself? Was there a specific moment you started to believe this lie?*

___

___

___

___

___

How has this lie affected you? *Has this lie led to certain choices? Has this lie held you back from opportunities or joy?*

How would your life change if you believed the truth instead of this lie?

Pick a memory verse to repeat to yourself whenever this lie pops into your head and write it here.

LIE:
My actions decide if I go to heaven.

TRUTH:
Jesus is the only way to salvation and heaven.

"I do not treat the grace of God as meaningless. For if keeping the law could make us right with God, then there was no need for Christ to die."
– *Galatians 2:21*

"God saved you by his grace when you believed. And you can't take credit for this; it is a gift from God."
– *Ephesians 2:8*

"For God made Christ, who never sinned, to be the offering for our sin, so that we could be made right with God through Christ."
– *2 Corinthians 5:21*

"There is salvation in no one else! God has given no other name under heaven by which we must be saved."
– *Acts 4:12*

From a young age, we are taught that we are in control of our actions, and it is our actions that dictate whether we are good or bad. It is true that we have free will, that we make our own choices, and that we decide our actions. However, there is only one choice that affects whether or not we go to heaven when we pass, and that is if we have accepted Jesus Christ as our Lord and Savior in our hearts. So much of our lives are lived in grey, but when it comes to salvation the answer is black and white. You are either saved through Jesus, or you are not. That may sound harsh, and I completely understand and empathize with wanting to believe that good people go to heaven and bad people do not. The problem with that thinking is that it makes us the judge and decider of who is "good" and who is "bad" when the only true judge is God. Romans 3:23 tells us that everyone has sinned and fallen short of God's glory, which means that in God's just and perfect eyes no human can be "good" because we are all sinful. This would be a horribly tragic thing to understand if it were not for the good news of Jesus Christ! In John 3:16–17, Jesus says, "For this is how God loved the world: He gave his one and only Son so that everyone who believes in him will not perish but have eternal life. God sent his Son into the world not to judge the world, but to save the world through him."

Encouragement

It will never be our day-to-day actions that decide if we earn a spot in heaven. This does not mean that our day-to-day actions mean nothing, however. Accepting Christ as your Lord and Savior gets you into heaven, but your actions decide your heavenly rewards. In Colossians 3:23–24, we are told to "work willingly at whatever you do, as though you were working for the Lord rather than for people. Remember that the Lord will give you an inheritance as your reward and that the Master you are serving is Christ."

Self-Study

How did this lie start? *Was it told to you or did you tell it to yourself? Was there a specific moment you started to believe this lie?*

____

____

____

____

____

____

____

____

____

____

How has this lie affected you? *Has this lie led to certain choices? Has this lie held you back from opportunities or joy?*

How would your life change if you believed the truth instead of this lie?

Pick a memory verse to repeat to yourself whenever this lie pops into your head and write it here.

LIE:
God is punishing me.

TRUTH:
God does not punish Christ-followers because their sins were paid for at the cross; God will discipline them if necessary, though.

"So now there is no condemnation for those who belong to Christ Jesus."
– *Romans 8:1*

"For no one is abandoned by the Lord forever. Though he brings grief, he also shows compassion because of the greatness of his unfailing love. For he does not enjoy hurting people or causing them sorrow."
– *Lamentations 3:31–33*

"He does not punish us for all our sins; he does not deal harshly with us, as we deserve."
– *Psalms 103:10*

It is true that God is just, and payment must be made for our sins. Thankfully, we serve a God that loves us so deeply that instead of giving us the wrath we deserve, he sent his son Jesus to pay the price of our sins so that we can live in a relationship with him. God does not punish his children; he may discipline, but he does not punish them.

God uses our circumstances, environment, relationships, and experiences to shape us into better people. God's correction is not from a place of anger or control, nor is it meant to be seen as a punishment. God's correction comes from loving us and wanting us to live fuller, happier lives. "My child don't reject the Lord's discipline, and don't be upset when he corrects you. For the Lord corrects those he loves, just as a father corrects a child in whom he delights" (Proverbs 3:11–12). I understand that discipline and correction may not seem like something you want to welcome with open arms, but these lessons come from a God who wants to place you on the best path and love you fully. That is the difference between discipline and punishment; discipline helps us to grow and guides us in the future, while punishment is retribution for an offense.

For those who are not saved, there are biblical instances where God does punish people far from him for their sins. This is because Jesus is unable to offer himself as sacrifice for the sins of those who do not have faith in him. If you are willing to accept Jesus into your heart, though, and repent of your sins, God will forgive every transgression. "If you openly declare that Jesus is Lord and believe in your heart that God raised him from the dead, you will be saved" (Romans 10:9).

It also needs to be stated that not all hardships are lessons from God. We live in a broken and sinful world that leaves no one unscathed. The beauty of our Lord, though, is that he can use anything to his glory.

Encouragement

Everyone has done things they are not proud of. Being human means mistakes are inevitable, but thankfully we are not the sum of our mistakes! Mistakes lead to growth and growth allows us to do better in the future. Instead of running or hiding from your past, raise your head high and own it. Unpopular fact: people are allowed to and often do change throughout their life. Who you were ten years ago, five years ago, or even yesterday does not have to dictate who you are today.

Self-Study

How did this lie start? *Was it told to you or did you tell it to yourself? Was there a specific moment you started to believe this lie?*

____

____

____

____

____

____

How has this lie affected you? *Has this lie led to certain choices? Has this lie held you back from opportunities or joy?*

How would your life change if you believed the truth instead of this lie?

Pick a memory verse to repeat to yourself whenever this lie pops into your head and write it here.

Shield of Faith

LIMITING GOD

We serve a big God! And when I say big, what I truly mean is limitless. We serve a God that can stop the sun in the sky (Joshua 10) who can part the sea (Exodus 14) and bring dry bones to life (Ezekiel 37). The power of God is profound, there is nothing our God cannot do! In knowing this, why is it that we continually choose to limit God with our doubt, disbelief, and lack of faith? In Matthew 17:20, Jesus said, "You don't have enough faith. I tell you the truth, if you had faith even as small as a mustard seed, you could say to this mountain, 'Move from here to there,' and it would move. Nothing would be impossible." If we would allow it, our faith has the power to move mountains! Yet so often we forget this power and choose to stay immersed in our circumstances. Why? Is it the fear of failure, are we afraid to hear "not yet," or worse, "no?"

It is true, not everything we ask of God will be granted or answered. But that does not mean that he does not hear our request or that he has forgotten us. We have a piece of the puzzle, while God sees the whole picture. Because of this God will sometimes make decisions that we will not understand, this side of heaven. If we choose to never ask though, we will never have the chance to receive it. Do not let fear stop you from obtaining the mercy, blessings, and miracles God wants to give you!

What are the lies that you have bought into that cause you to limit God? What has this world convinced you that God cannot do for you? We must stop allowing the walls of our minds to impede the purpose and potential that God has set forth for our lives. When we limit God, we lose—because limiting God limits ourselves. Choose today, right now, to put your faith in the God of miracles and you will begin to see how expansive the love, grace, and power of God is.

LIE:
God cannot use me.

TRUTH:
God can use anyone for good if they surrender to him.

"And we know that God causes everything to work together for the good of those who love God and are called according to his purpose for them."
–Romans 8:28

"And I am certain that God, who began the good work within you, will continue his work until it is finally finished on the day when Christ Jesus returns."
–Philippians 1:6

This has been, personally, one of the toughest lies I have had to destroy in my life. It is easy to believe that God can use other people, but when it comes to me a million excuses come crashing into my head as to why I am not equipped for the job. The truth, though, is that God does not call me or you to be qualified; he calls us to be obedient. Part of being obedient to God is having the faith to say yes in the uncertain. Yes, I will listen. Yes, I will follow. Yes, I will trust that you will prepare and supply me with whatever is needed to fulfill your purpose. Moses describes himself in Exodus 4:10 as "slow of speech and slow of tongue." Paul speaks in Acts 22:4 of how he "persecuted the followers of the way, hounding some to death, arresting both men and women and throwing them in prison." Despite their flaws and checkered pasts, God was still able to use Moses and Paul, not because they were perfect, but because they said yes. It is the same with you and me. If we spend our time recoiling inward, waiting for a guarantee before moving forward, we will never know the full extent of our potential. God can only use us if we surrender ourselves to his purpose.

Encouragement

Our flaws humanize us and help connect us to others. People struggle to relate to perfection because it isn't attainable for them, but seeing someone overcome the same sins they battle breeds hope. Sometimes the hardest part of saying yes is stepping out of your own way. Do not allow your unbelief in yourself to hold you back from saying yes to all God has for you.

Self-Study

How did this lie start? *Was it told to you or did you tell it to yourself? Was there a specific moment you started to believe this lie?*

How has this lie affected you? *Has this lie led to certain choices? Has this lie held you back from opportunities or joy?*

Is there a dream or passion you feel strongly about but have not pursued? What is holding you back?

How would your life change if you believed the truth instead of this lie?

Pick a memory verse to repeat to yourself whenever this lie pops into your head and write it here.

LIE:
God does not realize how bad my sins are.

TRUTH:
Your sins are not a secret, God knows them even before you commit them, and the blood of Jesus paid for them all.

"But if we confess our sins to him, he is faithful and just to forgive us our sins and to cleanse us from all wickedness."
–1 John 1:9

"This includes you who were once far away from God. You were his enemies, separated from him by your evil thoughts and actions. Yet now he has reconciled you to himself through the death of Christ in his physical body. As a result, he has brought you into his own presence, and you are holy and blameless as you stand before him without a single fault."
– Colossians 1:21-22

It is funny how we can logically understand that God is all-knowing, yet we somehow feel that in order to love us there must be things he is not aware of. We look at our sins through human eyes and cannot imagine how anyone could love us despite them. However, what we should be doing is recognizing that God knows it all—the good, the bad, the dark, the ugly—and still relentlessly pursues us so that we may feel his love. Not only that, because of Jesus's sacrifice on the cross when God looks at those of us who are born again, he sees perfection. If you do not yet know Jesus, God will see your sins, but the beauty of our heavenly Father is that he loves you even knowing everything you have done, are doing, and will do and he is waiting to accept you with open arms.

Jesus led by example and, as Christians, it is our mission to fully know Jesus so that we may emulate him. When Jesus was asked by his disciples how many times they should forgive others, his response gave us insight into how great his forgiveness of us is. "Then Peter came and said to him, 'Lord, how often shall my brother sin against me and I forgive him? Up to seven times?' Jesus said to him, 'I do not say to you, up to seven times, but up to seventy times seven'" (Matthew 18:21, 22). The point here is not to start a tally of every time you have to forgive someone. It is the opposite; Jesus knew Peter was not going to be able to keep track of whether he forgave someone 490 times. What Jesus was saying is that you should always forgive others because God always forgives you. There is no limit on God's love, grace, or forgiveness.

Encouragement

Along with God's forgiveness, it is also important to forgive yourself. We are not called to live a life where we continually punish ourselves for past sins. God does not want you to live in guilt; he wants you to repent so that you may walk in freedom and live in abundance. Just as God gives you grace, learn to be gracious with yourself. You are the only "you" you have, so be kind.

Self-Study

How did this lie start? *Was it told to you or did you tell it to yourself? Was there a specific moment you started to believe this lie?*

___

___

___

___

___

___

___

___

___

___

How has this lie affected you? *Has this lie led to certain choices? Has this lie held you back from opportunities or joy?*

How would your life change if you believed the truth instead of this lie?

Pick a memory verse to repeat to yourself whenever this lie pops into your head and write it here.

LIE:
My sins cannot be forgiven.

TRUTH:
When Jesus died on the cross he paid for every single sin—mine, yours, everyone's. His blood covers it all!

"Let the wicked change their ways and banish the very thought of doing wrong. Let them turn to the Lord that he may have mercy on them. Yes, turn to our God, for he will forgive generously."
– Isaiah 55:7

"Now repent of your sins and turn to God, so that your sins may be wiped away."
– Acts 3:19

"But if we confess our sins to him, he is faithful and just to forgive us our sins and to cleanse us from all wickedness."
– 1 John 1:9

God's forgiveness can be a really hard concept to wrap your head around. Often this is because we are unable to forgive ourselves, and if we cannot even forgive ourselves, why would God forgive us? It is important to understand that God does not use guilt or shame to teach lessons, nor does he require us to work for his forgiveness. Those are lies straight from the devil. Jesus says, in Luke 5:32, "I have come to call not those who think they are righteous, but those who know they are sinners and need to repent." There is no sin that cannot be forgiven if you are willing to repent of it.

Digging Deeper

"So I tell you, every sin and blasphemy can be forgiven—except blasphemy against the Holy Spirit, which will never be forgiven" (Matthew 12:31). Some people point to this verse when trying to prove they are beyond forgiveness as an explanation that God does not forgive all. Others live in fear that they have committed blasphemy against the Holy Spirit and therefore can never be forgiven.

Let us break it down: blasphemy of the Holy Spirit cannot be forgiven because in order to blasphemy the Spirit you have hardened your heart to the word and turned from Jesus. Meaning that though you have heard the Good News you do not accept it. Our God is just; therefore, our sins must be atoned for, which Jesus did for us by taking on our sins and dying on the cross so that his blood covers our transgressions. However, his selfless act only applies to those who are saved, who have accepted the gift of Jesus, allowing the Holy Spirit to enter them. Simply put, if you do not know Jesus he cannot pay for your sins. Essentially what is being said in Matthew 12:31 is that the sin of blasphemy against the Holy Spirit cannot be forgiven because the person who commits that sin is not saved and is unwilling to seek repentance.

Encouragement

Rejoice and take comfort in the fact that no matter how far you run or how deep you fall, God is waiting with open arms to embrace and love you fully! If you are willing to confess that Jesus is Lord, accept him into your heart as your savior, and repent, there is no sin that cannot be forgiven! The choice to be absolved of your sins and accepted completely regardless of your past is yours to make.

Self-Study

How did this lie start? *Was it told to you or did you tell it to yourself? Was there a specific moment you started to believe this lie?*

____

____

____

____

____

____

How has this lie affected you? *Has this lie led to certain choices? Has this lie held you back from opportunities or joy?*

What are the specific sins you believe God cannot forgive you for?

After writing out your list take a moment to pray, repenting of the sins on the list. Remember that by repenting it not only means that you are sorry for your actions, but that you will turn from your sinful ways. This does not mean you will forever be perfect; however, it does mean you are actively pursuing and applying the commandments of the Lord to your life.

How would your life change if you believed the truth instead of this lie?

Pick a memory verse to repeat to yourself whenever this lie pops into your head and write it here.

LIE:
God cannot fix my messy life.

TRUTH:
There is nothing God cannot fix if you turn to him.

"This means that anyone who belongs to Christ has become a new person. The old life is gone; a new life has begun!"
– 2 Corinthians 5:17

Face it, we all have messes somewhere in our lives. Whether it is a messy past or messy present, oftentimes mess is inescapable; being human is just messy. The wonderful thing is that our mess is often where God's light can shine brightest. By acknowledging your mess and surrendering it to God you allow him to step in and use the brokenness for good! Your mess can go from a dark secret to your testimony, or to how you relate to others and are able to help them.

When God pulls you out of a pit it is not just so that you can be better, it is so that you can reach back down into that pit and begin to help others out as well. Whatever your mess— porn, addiction, adultery, self-harm, debt, or even if you are just burnt out on life—God can transform your mess into peace. True joy and peace come not from having a perfect life, but from knowing that when things get hard and hectic you can lean into Christ and find space to breathe.

Encouragement

What we speak over ourselves matters. Try changing your perspective and your words from "I'm a mess" to "I'm human" and give yourself grace. By making simple changes in your phrasing overtime, it impacts how you see and feel about yourself. If you find it difficult to speak lovingly to yourself, try looking in the mirror and pretending your reflection is a friend of yours. The care we take when talking to our friends is the same care and kindness we need when speaking to ourselves.

Self-Study

How did this lie start? *Was it told to you or did you tell it to yourself? Was there a specific moment you started to believe this lie?*

How has this lie affected you? *Has this lie led to certain choices? Has this lie held you back from opportunities or joy?*

How would your life change if you believed the truth instead of this lie?

What are some common negative phrases you use to describe yourself and how can you reword them with grace? *For example, "I cannot do this" becomes "I will try" and "I'm so lazy" becomes "sometimes I need to rest."*

Pick a memory verse to repeat to yourself whenever this lie pops into your head and write it here.

LIE:
God will not answer my prayers.

TRUTH:
God hears and answers every prayer.

"You can pray for anything, and if you have faith, you will receive it."
– Matthew 21:22

"I tell you, you can pray for anything, and if you believe that you've received it, it will be yours."
– Mark 11:24

"Then you will call upon Me and come and pray to Me, and I will listen to you."
– Jeremiah 29:12 (NASB)

"But if you remain in me and my words remain in you, you may ask for anything you want, and it will be granted!"
– John 15:7

"And we are confident that he hears us whenever we ask for anything that pleases him. And since we know he hears us when we make our requests, we also know that he will give us what we ask for."
– 1 John 5:14-15

The Bible is clear that God hears and answers our prayers, so why then does it sometimes seem that he is silent? James 4:2–3 tells us "Yet you don't have what you want because you don't ask God for it. And even when you ask, you don't get it because your motives are all wrong—you want only what will give you pleasure." Too often this is the case with our prayers. If God is not answering your prayers, you first need to evaluate the true intentions of your prayer and whether or not those intentions line up with God's word.

If after reflecting, you know your prayer aligns with God's word then consider that God's timing is quite different from ours. What we interpret as God not answering may just be that the right time has not come yet. A biblical example of this is Sarah, who waited twenty-five years before her prayer of having a child was answered.

Beyond this we need to understand that "no" could be his answer. We do not have access to all the information; God does. For reasons we cannot know, we may not always get a "yes" even when it seems we should. If God has answered your prayer with a "no," try to understand that whether we can see it or not he is making the best possible decision.

It is also important to make sure that you are not blocking your own prayer. First John 3:21–22 says, "Dear friends, if we don't feel guilty, we can come to God with bold confidence. And we will receive from him whatever we ask because we obey him and do the things that please him." Is it perhaps your un-forgiveness of others or your unrepented sins that are hindering your blessing? When we go to God with requests, we first have to search our hearts. "Be reconciled with Him, and be at peace; thereby good will come to you" (Job 22:21, NASB).

Encouragement

Take time to examine your heart, writing down the reasons and intentions behind your prayers. Waiting will wear you down if you let it; be intentional and stay strong in your faith knowing that all things are possible with our God!

Self-Study

How did this lie start? *Was it told to you or did you tell it to yourself? Was there a specific moment you started to believe this lie?*

___

___

___

___

___

How has this lie affected you? *Has this lie led to certain choices? Has this lie held you back from opportunities or joy?*

How would your life change if you believed the truth instead of this lie?

Write down your current prayers and the date. Whenever a prayer is answered come back to this section and mark it out with the date.

Pick a memory verse to repeat to yourself whenever this lie pops into your head and write it here.

LIE:
My troubles are too small for God to care.

TRUTH:
God loves you and cares about the things that trouble your heart.

"What is the price of two sparrows—one copper coin? But not a single sparrow can fall to the ground without your Father knowing it."
– *Matthew 10:29*

First Peter 5:7 prompts us to give all our worries and cares to God because he cares for us. It does not say give some of your worries and cares. It does not say if your problems seem big enough to warrant "bothering" God. It says give ALL your worries and cares. And the reason we are to give them all is that God cares for us and, therefore, wants to hear the things that trouble our minds and hearts. Further proof that nothing is too small for God is found in Philippians 4:6, "Don't worry about anything; instead, pray about **everything**. Tell God what you need, and thank him for all he has done." We are not told to only pray about the big things that happen in our lives. God walks with us through everything, the good, the bad, the small, the grand, and everything in between. He cares for us at every moment.

Encouragement

Jesus is our greatest friend! You are not a burden to him; he does not ignore you or need space. When it comes to God, there is always an open invitation to engage in true intimacy.

Self-Study

How did this lie start? *Was it told to you or did you tell it to yourself? Was there a specific moment you started to believe this lie?*

____

____

How has this lie affected you? *Has this lie led to certain choices? Has this lie held you back from opportunities or joy?*

How would your life change if you believed the truth instead of this lie?

Pick a memory verse to repeat to yourself whenever this lie pops into your head and write it here.

Sword of the Spirit

SUICIDE, SELF-HARM, & ABUSE

Trauma, depression, and anxiety are cultivators of suicidal thoughts and self-harm. Our minds can take us to very dark places that seem impossible to pull ourselves out of. However, beauty, comfort, and peace come when you realize that you were never intended to single-handedly pull yourself out of a hole. God wants to help you; he wants to lend you his strength and he wants you to be surrounded by the support of his followers cheering you on. Take hope in knowing that you do not have to go through this alone because there is help.

Foremost, know that Jesus loves you and can grant you peace. "Then you will experience God's peace, which exceeds anything we can understand. His peace will guard your hearts and minds as you live in Christ Jesus" (Philippians 4:7). Then there is the church community that can surround you and help to carry your burdens. "Share each other's burdens, and in this way obey the law of Christ" (Galatians 6:2). And beyond that, there are advocates, counselors, and therapists that can guide you in healthy ways to navigate your feelings. "Where there is no guidance the people fall, but in an abundance of counselors, there is victory" (Proverbs 11:14, NASB).

The enemy will try and convince you that you must keep your pain bottled inside. That no one wants to hear or be bothered by it. That is a lie! Please do not keep these feelings buried inside of you. "The light shines in the darkness, and the darkness has not overcome it" (John 1:5, ESV). Truth is light, and when you put forth your light the darkness flees.

If you or a loved one are struggling with thoughts of suicide, please reach out to a counselor for guidance or call the National Suicide Prevention Lifeline at 800-273-8255 for help.

LIE:
Others would be better off if I were dead.

TRUTH:
God created you to walk this earth with love and a purpose!

"For we are God's masterpiece. He has created us anew in Christ Jesus, so we can do the good things he planned for us long ago."
– *Ephesians 2:10*

"But you belong to God, my dear children. You have already won a victory over those people, because the Spirit who lives in you is greater than the spirit who lives in the world."
– *1 John 4:4*

This is one of the darkest lies the devil can plant in your mind, and it *is* a lie. Even if you have no one else on this earth who loves you, God does, and he created you uniquely with a purpose. No matter your circumstance, you have the ability to affect and inject those around you with joy, strength, and positivity. When God created you, he mapped out a life that includes a path of planting seeds and blessing people throughout your time on Earth. We are lucky to witness some of these seeds bear fruit into wonderful blessings to those around us. However, many of the blessings that we put into motion go unbeknownst to us. If you choose suicide you are not only taking away the option for things in your own life to get better, but you are also denying people you would have come in contact with the blessings you were meant to give. "The generous will prosper; those who refresh others will themselves be refreshed" (Proverbs 11:25).

Encouragement

The devil wants to steal your power by making you believe this does not apply to you and that you cannot be a blessing but in Jesus's name, I declare that this lie is cast out from your mind! Romans 8:37 tells us that "overwhelming victory is ours through Christ." Our God is stronger than the devil,

He is greater than the darkness surrounding you. Stand up, and claim your victory!

Self-Study

How did this lie start? *Was it told to you or did you tell it to yourself? Was there a specific moment you started to believe this lie?*

How has this lie affected you? *Has this lie led to certain choices? Has this lie held you back from opportunities or joy?*

How would your life change if you believed the truth instead of this lie?

Create a list of people you have had a positive impact on, big or small, in their life. *If you cannot think of any names in the moment, that is okay! Look at this as an opportunity to start impacting people today! Examples: opening the door for a stranger, complimenting someone, helping with a project.*

Refer to this list when you start to sink into the lie that others would be better off without you.

Pick a memory verse to repeat to yourself whenever this lie pops into your head and write it here.

LIE:
I should give up.

TRUTH:
There is no circumstance the Lord will not bring you out of if you give him the reins.

"Then Jesus said, "Come to me, all of you who are weary and carry heavy burdens, and I will give you rest."
– Matthew 11:28

"So let's not get tired of doing what is good. At just the right time we will reap a harvest of blessing if we don't give up."
– Galatians 6:9

"That is why we never give up. Though our bodies are dying, our spirits are being renewed every day. For our present troubles are small and won't last very long. Yet they produce for us a glory that vastly outweighs them and will last forever! So we don't look at the troubles we can see now; rather, we fix our gaze on things that cannot be seen. For the things we see now will soon be gone, but the things we cannot see will last forever."
– 2 Corinthians 4:16–18

Do not give up! You are loved and your God and his angels are in heaven rooting for you! Life is hard, it is messy, and it hurts, but it is worth living. If you quit now you will miss out on all the plans God has for you. Jeremiah 29:11 states "'For I know the plans I have for you,' says the Lord. 'They are plans for good and not for disaster, to give you a future and a hope.'" Whatever the circumstances of your life may be, please do not give up. Reach out to friends, family, your church community, or a specialist. I guarantee there are people that want to help you carry your burdens; find them.

Encouragement

If this life is not what you expected or want, press into God. Use your time here to pursue him, and to build up your storehouse of treasures in heaven. Matthew 6:19–20 tells us, "Don't store up treasures here on earth, where moths eat them and rust destroys them, and where thieves break in and steal. Store your treasures in heaven, where moths and rust cannot destroy, and thieves do not break in and steal." Luke 21:19 assures us that "by standing firm, you will win your souls." Keep going, endure and know that Jesus loves you and by accepting him you are promised a place of peace and joy in heaven. In 1 Peter 1:4 we are told "we have a priceless inheritance—an inheritance that is kept in heaven for you, pure and undefiled, beyond the reach of change and decay."

Self-Study

How did this lie start? *Was it told to you or did you tell it to yourself? Was there a specific moment you started to believe this lie?*

____

____

____

____

____

____

____

____

How has this lie affected you? *Has this lie led to certain choices? Has this lie held you back from opportunities or joy?*

____

____

____

____

Write down bad seasons in your life that you are no longer in. *For example: a toxic work environment that you have left for a new job.*

Refer to this as proof that circumstances change even when we feel there is no light at the end of the tunnel.

How would your life change if you believed the truth instead of this lie?

Pick a memory verse to repeat to yourself whenever this lie pops into your head and write it here.

LIE:
I am a mistake.

TRUTH:
God does not make mistakes; he created you with joy and meaning.

"He is the Rock; his deeds are perfect. Everything he does is just and fair. He is a faithful God who does no wrong; how just and upright he is!"
– Deuteronomy 32:4

"'For I know the plans I have for you,' says the Lord. 'They are plans for good and not for disaster, to give you a future and a hope.'"
– Jeremiah 29:11

It is worth repeating; God does not make mistakes. Everything created by him, which includes all humans, has a purpose and a path that he has laid out. "For we are God's masterpiece. He has created us anew in Christ Jesus, so we can do the good things he planned for us long ago" (Ephesians 2:10). People do not plan for mistakes, you were carefully planned and given a purpose. God intentionally creating you makes you far from a mistake, it makes you loved fully. As humans we are flawed and bound to make errors, but making mistakes does not mean that we are a mistake. We will all fall short or suffer at times. No matter how deep we plummet, or how broken we become, though, God can restore us fully!

Encouragement

God put careful thought and planning into creating you; you are here for a purpose and you are so very loved! Psalms 139:13 clearly tells us that God deliberately created every part of you and I; "You made all the delicate, inner parts of my body and knit me together in my mother's womb." You are not a haphazardly made craft project. You were knit together with delicate precision because our God decided the world needed you.

Self-Study

How did this lie start? *Was it told to you or did you tell it to yourself? Was there a specific moment you started to believe this lie?*

How has this lie affected you? *Has this lie led to certain choices? Has this lie held you back from opportunities or joy?*

How would your life change if you believed the truth instead of this lie?

Pick a memory verse to repeat to yourself whenever this lie pops into your head and write it here.

LIE:
Life is not worth living.

TRUTH:
Life has ups and downs, but you can find lasting peace through it all in Jesus.

"For everything there is a season, a time for every activity under heaven."
– *Ecclesiastes 3:1*

"Then you will experience God's peace, which exceeds anything we can understand. His peace will guard your hearts and minds as you live in Christ Jesus."
– *Philippians 4:7*

There are times when living can feel insufferable, and I want so badly to tell you that being a Christian protects you from the pain of the world. But that would not be the truth. Being a Christian does not mean life will be without problems, Jesus warns us in John 16:33 that "here on earth you will have many trials and sorrows." God does not make light of the fact that life will be hard. In the hardship though he does not say to give up, instead, he instructs us in Matthew 24:13 that "the one who endures to the end will be saved." He goes on to encourage us in John 8:12 saying "I am the light of the world. If you follow me, you won't have to walk in darkness, because you will have the light that leads to life."

Yes, life is hard, but when your strength to go on runs out, borrow from God's surplus. If you begin to feel overwhelmed, push into God, seek his peace and comfort. In John 14:27 Jesus says, "I am leaving you with a gift—peace of mind and heart. And the peace I give is a gift the world cannot give." Being a Christ-follower does not take away your hardship, it gives you access to joy even in the midst of your trials.

Encouragement

God knows your pain. Psalm 56:8 tells us, "You keep track of all my sorrows. You have collected all my tears in your bottle. You have recorded each one in your book." Not only is he aware of your pain, he promises to bring good from it. In Romans 8:28 we find the following: "We know that God causes everything to work together for the good of those who love God." Do not cut your life short before God is able to turn your sorrow into triumph, your hurt into a platform to help and bless others. God's vision for you is so much greater than you can imagine, and it is worth living for.

Self-Study

How did this lie start? *Was it told to you or did you tell it to yourself? Was there a specific moment you started to believe this lie?*

____

____

____

____

____

____

____

____

How has this lie affected you? *Has this lie led to certain choices? Has this lie held you back from opportunities or joy?*

____

____

____

____

____

How would your life change if you believed the truth instead of this lie?

What are some goals you would like to achieve in life? What steps can you take today to begin your journey?

Pick a memory verse to repeat to yourself whenever this lie pops into your head and write it here.

Write down a list of action steps that you can take when suicidal thoughts enter your mind. *This could include the Suicide Prevention Lifeline number, contacting your counselor, calling a trusted friend, or trying some of the self-harm alternatives in the back of the book.*

LIE:
I am too far-off track to come back.

TRUTH:
God meets us where we are.

"For God was in Christ, reconciling the world to himself, no longer counting people's sins against them. And he gave us this wonderful message of reconciliation."
– 2 Corinthians 5:19

"And when he has found it, he will joyfully carry it home on his shoulders. When he arrives, he will call together his friends and neighbors, saying, 'Rejoice with me because I have found my lost sheep.'"
– Luke 15:5–6

Other than your own choosing there is nothing that can keep you separated from the love of God. People will judge you, the world may try to force you to live in your past, and the devil will use your mistakes to mislead you;

> "But God is so rich in mercy, and he loved us so much, that even though we were dead because of our sins, he gave us life when he raised Christ from the dead. (It is only by God's grace that you have been saved!) For he raised us from the dead along with Christ and seated us with him in the heavenly realms because we are united with Christ Jesus. So God can point to us in all future ages as examples of the incredible wealth of his grace and kindness toward us, as shown in all he has done for us who are united with Christ Jesus. God saved you by his grace when you believed. And you cannot take credit for this; it is a gift from God. Salvation is not a reward for the good things we have done, so none of us can boast about it. For we are God's masterpiece. He has created us anew

> in Christ Jesus, so we can do the good things he planned for us long ago" (Ephesians 2:4–10).

It is not our actions, good or bad, that decide our fate. Salvation comes from a relationship with Jesus. We carry so much shame with our sins, but our sins are why God sent us Jesus. God so desperately wanted to be close with us that he gave his only begotten son so that we may be with him. God knows every darkness in your heart and every low you have hit trying to escape or cope, yet still he wants you. You are not too far off track, you are in exactly the right moment to turn from your past and start a future following God.

Encouragement

"In the same way, there is more joy in heaven over one lost sinner who repents and returns to God than over ninety-nine others who are righteous and haven't strayed away" (Luke 15:7). God recognizes your hardships and rejoices when through it all you still choose to worship him.

Self-Study

How did this lie start? *Was it told to you or did you tell it to yourself? Was there a specific moment you started to believe this lie?*

____

____

____

____

____

____

____

____

How has this lie affected you? *Has this lie led to certain choices? Has this lie held you back from opportunities or joy?*

How would your life change if you believed the truth instead of this lie?

Pick a memory verse to repeat to yourself whenever this lie pops into your head and write it here.

LIE:
It helps me to cut myself.

TRUTH:
Cutting yourself not only hurts you, but it also hurts God.

If you are using cutting as a coping mechanism please speak with a counselor about healthy alternatives and read the self-harm alternatives section in the back of this book.

"Don't you realize that your body is the temple of the Holy Spirit, who lives in you and was given to you by God? You do not belong to yourself, for God bought you with a high price. So you must honor God with your body."
– *1 Corinthians 6:19–20*

"Your kindness will reward you, but your cruelty will destroy you."
– *Proverbs 11:17*

There are many reasons people cut themselves. Temporarily it may make you feel in control or give you an emotional release, but it is a temporary high that does colossal damage to your body, self-worth, mental health, and soul. Self-harm is often shrouded in secrecy and shame; neither of which are from God. The devil wants you to believe that you cannot share your pain with others because they will get mad or they will not understand. The reality is though that the devil does not want you to share because when you do, he loses control. Stop giving away your power. Deep down you know that harming yourself does not solve your hurts, it does not process your pain, it is a momentary outlet that leaves you with guilt that only adds to your anguish.

Please know that you are deserving and worthy of others respecting your body and you are deserving and worthy of respecting and loving yourself. You were created and are loved by God and just as it breaks his heart for others to hurt you, it breaks his heart when you hurt yourself. You are important and it matters that you treat yourself with kindness in both your words and actions. Whether it is for punishment, pain, or release, it does not help you to cut yourself. What will help you is cloaking yourself in the love and grace of God while reaching out to others to help you explore healthy ways to work through your pain.

Encouragement

You can and will overcome this! When the urge to cut creeps in, lean into God, for his strength cannot fail! "For God has not given us a spirit of fear and timidity, but of power, love, and self-discipline" (2 Timothy 1:7). Again, I want to encourage you to seek outside guidance from a professional who can help you by providing healthy coping options that you can use in conjunction with prayer and your faith. Do not allow the world's judgment or the devil to keep you from living a healthy life.

Self-Study

How did this lie start? *Was it told to you or did you tell it to yourself? Was there a specific moment you started to believe this lie?*

____

____

____

____

____

____

____

____

____

____

____

____

How has this lie affected you? *Has this lie led to certain choices? Has this lie held you back from opportunities or joy?*

How would your life change if you believed the truth instead of this lie?

Turn to the *Self Harm Alternatives* section of the book. Using it as a reference, pick three alternatives to try next time you have the urge to harm yourself.

1. ______________________________

2. ______________________________

3. ______________________________

Pick a memory verse to repeat to yourself whenever this lie pops into your head and write it here.

____

____

____

____

____

____

____

____

____

____

LIE:
I was raped so sex does not matter anymore.

TRUTH:
God does not blame you for the sins of your rapist.

> "But if the man meets the engaged woman out in the country, and he rapes her, then only the man must die. Do nothing to the young woman; she has committed no crime worthy of death. She is as innocent as a murder victim."
> – *Deuteronomy 22:25–26*

I am so sorry that you were violated and, because there are both women and men who need to hear this, please know that making choices for your survival is not the same as consent. I pray that you do not see yourself as a reflection of your assault/abuse but instead that you are fully healed through Jesus, seeing your true value in his eyes. Being raped in no way diminishes your value or worth as a person. As said in Deuteronomy, as the victim you are innocent. Any shame or guilt that you carry from this assault comes straight from the devil. Whether you are a female or male survivor of sexual assault/rape, God does not hold you accountable for the sins committed against you. "For we are each responsible for our own conduct" (Galatians 6:5).

The heaviness and all-consuming pain of rape is recognized by God as he equates the act to murder "Do nothing to the young woman; she has committed no crime worthy of death. She is as innocent as a murder victim" (Deuteronomy 22:26). He knows the effects of sexual immorality on our minds, hearts, and bodies, warning us in 1 Corinthians 6:18 to "run from sexual sin! No other sin so clearly affects the body as this one does. For sexual immorality is a sin against your own body." God does not tell you this to shame you, He wants to make you aware of how precious your body is and that it should be respected. You matter and your past sexual history does not take away from the fact that you are worth waiting for.

Encouragement

The thoughts, words, and actions of another do not affect your worth. You were not called to walk in shame, guilt, or fear. You are precious and what you choose to do with your present and future matter. "He led them from the darkness and deepest gloom; he snapped their chains" (Psalm 107:14).

Digging Deeper

One of the reasons so much emphasis is placed on sexual immorality throughout the Bible is because God understands how devastating assault and rape are emotionally, mentally, and physically. God chose to compare rape to murder because he understands the toll and the heaviness of the crime.

Deuteronomy can be a hard book to navigate when you do not understand the culture, context, and laws of that period. This book is often misrepresented and misquoted in an effort to attack God's character. As a survivor, I myself have been challenged by some asking why I would believe in a God that made victims marry their rapist. As a newer Christian, this question shocked me, but it is a perfect example of why it is so important to know and research your Bible. If I had not been willing to sit down and learn for myself, I could have forever believed this twisted perception of God. If you read carefully, with an open heart, and do your research you will find that the commands of God regarding sexual purity and rape, in the context and time period they were given, were to protect the victim/survivor.

Thankfully, times have changed drastically, and women are now able to live successful lives and provide for themselves. However, in the times of the Old Testament it would have been extremely difficult for a woman to survive without a husband. Beyond the devastating effects of the rape itself, the act also took away any opportunity of future marriage proposals (a.k.a. food and shelter). Therefore, God commands that a rapist must pay a bride's price for the woman and marry her without ever having the option to divorce her (Deuteronomy 22:28-29). At that time being a divorcee would have made her an outcast of society. This is God holding rapists accountable for their actions. This is God saying that you do not just get to walk in, detonate a bomb, and then walk away. God does not give the rapist a choice in the marriage proposal, but he does give the victim/survivor a choice. God does not say that the woman must marry her rapist. God does not punish or shame the victim/survivor. God lays out laws that ensure that sexual assault and rape victims/survivors are not forced into a life of destitution because of the assault.

Self-Study

How did this lie start? *Was it told to you or did you tell it to yourself? Was there a specific moment you started to believe this lie?*

____

____

____

____

____

____

____

____

How has this lie affected you? *Has this lie led to certain choices? Has this lie held you back from opportunities or joy?*

____

____

____

____

____

____

How would your life change if you believed the truth instead of this lie?

Pick a memory verse to repeat to yourself whenever this lie pops into your head and write it here.

LIE:
I deserved to be treated badly.

TRUTH:
You should be treated with love.

"Love each other with genuine affection and take delight in honoring each other."
– Romans 12:10

"This is my commandment: Love each other in the same way I have loved you."
– John 15:12

"Do to others as you would like them to do to you."
– Luke 6:31

"Owe nothing to anyone—except for your obligation to love one another. If you love your neighbor, you will fulfill the requirements of God's law."
– Romans 13:8

Whether you are a Christian or a non-believer, and regardless of what you and all of us truly deserve, God has commanded you be treated with kindness. "Therefore, whenever we have the opportunity, we should do good to everyone" (Galatians 6:10). It is stated multiple times throughout the Bible how God wants us to treat others, and in turn how he wants others to treat us, which is with love. If you are a Christian, it is God's law that you show love to everyone, regardless of their beliefs, words or actions. This does not mean that you are stuck with people who are hurting you. You are still able to have love for someone while placing safe boundaries. If setting limits is something you struggle with I would strongly encourage you to read the book *Boundaries* by Dr. Henry Cloud and Dr. John Townsend.

If you are not a believer, and whether you choose to show others love or not, you fall under the umbrella of God's law and should be shown love. "Love does no wrong to others, so love fulfills the requirements of God's law"

(Romans 13:10).

We are called to love our neighbors and our neighbors are called to love us. When God calls us to love everyone that does not just mean everyone we like, it includes our enemies. "But to you who are willing to listen, I say, love your enemies! Do good to those who hate you" (Luke 6:27). In God's eyes, even our enemies are due our kindness. If he wants it for your enemies, think how much more he wants it for you!

Encouragement

You are worthy, you are enough, and you should accept nothing short of being treated with love. You have the right to protect yourself physically, emotionally, and mentally. Loving others does not require you to lose yourself to them. Someone does not have to actively participate in your life for you to love and pray over them. Discover and place the boundaries that are needed to keep yourself safe.

Self-Study

How did this lie start? *Was it told to you or did you tell it to yourself? Was there a specific moment you started to believe this lie?*

____

How has this lie affected you? *Has this lie led to certain choices? Has this lie held you back from opportunities or joy?*

How would your life change if you believed the truth instead of this lie?

Pick a memory verse to repeat to yourself whenever this lie pops into your head and write it here.

LIE:
I must have done something wrong if God let me get hurt.

TRUTH:
God gave us free will and there are people who use that free will to commit horrible acts, but their actions are not a reflection of you.

"And when sins have been forgiven, there is no need to offer any more sacrifices."
– *Hebrews 10:18*

"The LORD is compassionate and merciful, slow to get angry and filled with unfailing love. He will not constantly accuse us, nor remain angry forever. He does not punish us for all our sins; he does not deal harshly with us, as we deserve."
– *Psalm 103:8-10*

I fully understand and acknowledge the need to blame yourself or someone else for your pain; I have been there. The problem with blame is that it can often become our main focus. If we are not careful, blame can turn into hate and hate will manifest, spread, and destroy. The need to understand the "why" behind our pain is universal. However, the why is not always clear. What is clear is that we live in a sinful and broken world where hurt people continue to hurt other people in a vicious cycle in which only the devil excels.

Please know and accept that the trauma you have endured is not your fault. You are not responsible for the abuse, assault, or pain someone else chooses to inflict. Yes, you have sinned in your past and probably made many mistakes, as we all have, but that does not justify the harmful actions of another toward you. All of us have fallen short, the only perfect person was Jesus (Romans 3:10 & 3:23).

God uses discipline (not abuse), redirection, and conviction to help us grow from our mistakes. Satan uses sin, abuse, and torment. The devil wants you to think it is your fault, he wants to entrap you in his prison of lies where you stay paralyzed by fear, shame, and anger. He will do anything to succeed in immobilizing you from your full power in leading the life God wants for you.

Ultimately though, who you decide to give the power to is your choice. In no way does that mean healing is easy, because it is not. Healing is a long, often slow process with many setbacks. You are worthy of the process though! You are worthy of the time, commitment, grace, and love it takes to heal! Our God is a God who restores, "he heals the brokenhearted and bandages their wounds" (Psalms 147:3). Stop carrying your burden alone, give it to God and he will work your pain for good (Romans 8:28).

Encouragement

Your past does not give anyone the right to cause you pain. It is common for abusers to place blame on the people they hurt. But hurting you was their choice, and no matter what they claim, your actions do not justify their choice to be an abuser. The guilt you are feeling is not from God. Our God is not a shamer. He is a chain breaker and he is waiting to help you walk in full freedom from your past.

Self-Study

How did this lie start? *Was it told to you or did you tell it to yourself? Was there a specific moment you started to believe this lie?*

____

____

____

____

____

____

____

____

How has this lie affected you? *Has this lie led to certain choices? Has this lie held you back from opportunities or joy?*

How would your life change if you believed the truth instead of this lie?

Pick a memory verse to repeat to yourself whenever this lie pops into your head and write it here.

LIE:
My pain is God's fault.

TRUTH:
Your pain is the result of a sinful world.

"When Adam sinned, sin entered the world. Adam's sin brought death, so death spread to everyone, for everyone sinned."
– Romans 5:12

"For the sinful nature is always hostile to God. It never did obey God's laws, and it never will. That's why those who are still under the control of their sinful nature can never please God."
– Romans 8:7-8

" He comforts us in all our troubles so that we can comfort others. When they are troubled, we will be able to give them the same comfort God has given us."
– 2 Corinthians 1:4

"The Lord is close to the brokenhearted; he rescues those whose spirits are crushed."
– Psalm 34:18

The devil works extremely hard to spread this lie because it is one of the most beneficial to him. But our pain is not from God, it is an effect of the imperfect broken world we live in. When God first designed our world, it was perfect. We, as people, chose to introduce sin into the mix (Genesis 2:4–3:24). We were able to make that choice because God gives us free will. The reason the gift of free will is so important is that it shows God's heart in allowing us to choose to love and serve him instead of being forced.

Free will allows us to make our own choices. Unfortunately, though, with free will also comes the option to make bad decisions. Since God does not interfere with our free will the bad decisions of others often cause pain to themselves and those around them. I cannot pretend to know your pain, perhaps it was of your own making, or maybe it was the cruelty of others.

What I do know with certainty, however, is that the pain we experience is not God's fault.

Jesus tells us in John 10:10 "the thief (devil) comes only to steal and kill and destroy; I came so that they would have life and have it abundantly" (NASB). Projecting anger that should be directed at the devil and sin onto God will only amplify your pain. God is our healer and until we understand that he accepts us at our darkest and wants to give us comfort we will not be truly restored.

Encouragement

If you are reading this shrinking in your seat because you realize that you have wrongfully blamed, gotten angry at, or even hated God for your pain I encourage you to take a deep breath and release that guilt. Guilt is not a tool of God; it is a chain of the devil. There is nothing that you ask forgiveness and repent of that God will not forgive. Do not let guilt or shame drive you from our God who so desperately wants to dote on you.

Self-Study

How did this lie start? *Was it told to you or did you tell it to yourself? Was there a specific moment you started to believe this lie?*

____

____

____

____

____

____

____

____

____

How has this lie affected you? *Has this lie led to certain choices? Has this lie held you back from opportunities or joy?*

What pain in your life have you blamed God for?

How would your life change if you believed the truth instead of this lie?

Pick a memory verse to repeat to yourself whenever this lie pops into your head and write it here.

Belt of Truth

SELF-TALK

We live in a culture of consumerism that continually floods us with messages about what to eat, what diet to try, what to wear, what our clothing size should be, what our body should look like, how we should speak, how our family should look, how our home should look, what products to buy, and on and on and on. It has become so easy to buy into this culture and begin to feel that if you are not part of the latest social media trend that you are somehow less-than. We look at the highlight reels of others and compare our mess to their perfectly lit and obsessively edited images. And in doing so we become our own worst critics.

Many of us speak worse of ourselves than we ever would of a friend or even an enemy. How we talk to ourselves and what we let fill our mind matters because it sets the tone for our day, attitude, and self-image. You spend more time with yourself than anyone else on Earth. Meaning, more than anyone else, you have the greatest opportunity to speak love and life over yourself. "Death and life are in the power of the tongue, and those who love it will eat its fruit" (Proverbs 18:21, NASB).

I pray that by breaking down the following lies surrounding self-talk, chains are broken and you are able to see yourself through the eyes of Jesus with love and grace. "To acquire wisdom is to love yourself; people who cherish understanding will prosper" (Proverbs 19:8). The world is harsh enough to all of us; be kind to yourself.

LIE:
I have to be perfect.

TRUTH:
Jesus was the only perfect person to walk the earth, we all fall short of the glory.

"I don't mean to say that I have already achieved these things or that I have already reached perfection. But I press on to possess that perfection for which Christ Jesus first possessed me. No, dear brothers and sisters, I have not achieved it, but I focus on this one thing: Forgetting the past and looking forward to what lies ahead"
– *Philippians 3:12–13*

"For everyone has sinned; we all fall short of God's glorious standard."
– *Romans 3:23*

Do not make yourself miserable pursuing an impossible standard. How do I know perfection is out of reach for us all? Because the Bible clearly states it: "Not a single person on earth is always good and never sins" (Ecclesiastes 7:20). Jesus was, and forever will be the only perfect person. Thankfully though, your worth is not determined by perfection.

We serve a gracious and loving God who is quick to forgive our mistakes and shortcomings. You do not have to be perfect for God or anyone else to love you and you do not need to be perfect to succeed. Yes, failure sucks, but it also offers an opportunity for growth and betterment if you allow it. Grant your failures and mistakes permission to mold you into a better version of yourself. Process them so that you may learn, but do not sit in them so long that you become stuck.

Encouragement

Instead of striving to be flawless, try and dissect where this belief that you should be perfect came from, so that you may release yourself from the bondage of this lie. Were mistakes not accepted in your home or are you trying to meet someone's expectations? Dig into the self-study below to find the root of this lie.

Self-Study

How did this lie start? *Was it told to you or did you tell it to yourself? Was there a specific moment you started to believe this lie?*

____

____

____

____

____

____

____

____

How has this lie affected you? *Has this lie led to certain choices? Has this lie held you back from opportunities or joy?*

____

____

____

____

____

____

____

____

How would your life change if you believed the truth instead of this lie?

Pick a memory verse to repeat to yourself whenever this lie pops into your head and write it here.

LIE:
I cannot change.

TRUTH:
God can transform and renew you.

"For God has not given us a spirit of fear and timidity, but of power, love, and self-discipline."
– 2 Timothy 1:7

"This means that anyone who belongs to Christ has become a new person. The old life is gone; a new life has begun!"
– 2 Corinthians 5:17

For some change happens in an instant. But for many, transformation is a long process. "But we all, with unveiled faces, looking as in a mirror at the glory of the Lord, are being transformed into the same image from glory to glory, just as from the Lord, the Spirit" (2 Corinthians 3:18). Just because something takes time it does not mean there is no progression. Allow yourself grace in all seasons but especially in seasons of change. Lean into God and borrow from his strength for self-control.

Know that you are not alone in your struggles, temptation is something everyone faces, but you are strong enough to stay the path. "The temptations in your life are no different from what others experience. And God is faithful. He will not allow the temptation to be more than you can stand. When you are tempted, he will show you a way out so that you can endure" (1 Corinthians 10:13). If you are a Christian, God equipped you with everything necessary to change your old ways when he gave you the Holy Spirit. If you have hit a wall and do not know how to pray for transformation, the Bible tells us "now in the same way the Spirit also helps our weakness; for we do not know what to pray for as we should, but the Spirit Himself intercedes for us with groanings too deep for words" (Romans 8:26, NASB). Do not be discouraged if you have trouble asking for help or putting into words your needs and desires, because the Holy Spirit is praying on your behalf.

Encouragement

People change every day. Our circumstances and experiences are constantly molding us into new versions of ourselves. None of us will leave this life the same as when we entered it. You are not an exception; you are capable of change. "And I will give you a new heart, and I will put a new spirit in you. I will take out your stony, stubborn heart and give you a tender, responsive heart" (Ezekiel 36:26).

Self-Study

How did this lie start? *Was it told to you or did you tell it to yourself? Was there a specific moment you started to believe this lie?*

____

____

____

____

____

____

____

____

____

How has this lie affected you? *Has this lie led to certain choices? Has this lie held you back from opportunities or joy?*

____

____

____

Spend some time thinking about the person you were ten years ago and comparing that to the person you are currently. How have you changed?

Refer to this list when you believe you are incapable of change.

How would your life change if you believed the truth instead of this lie?

Pick a memory verse to repeat to yourself whenever this lie pops into your head and write it here.

LIE:
I am ugly.

TRUTH:
You were made in the image of God and are beautiful in his sight.

"But the Lord said to Samuel, "Don't judge by his appearance or height, for I have rejected him. The Lord doesn't see things the way you see them. People judge by outward appearance, but the Lord looks at the heart."
– 1 Samuel 16:7

"Yet God has made everything beautiful for its own time. He has planted eternity in the human heart, but even so, people cannot see the whole scope of God's work from beginning to end."
– Ecclesiastes 3:11

"So God created human beings in his own image. In the image of God he created them; male and female he created them."
– Genesis 1:27

In this day of social media, photo-shop, and filters, "beauty" has become an unrealistic standard for all of us. Physical beauty is in the eye of the beholder, it is different everywhere you go and has changed numerous times throughout history. Society puts so much pressure on outward beauty. But God knows that outward beauty is fleeting and does not always reflect the true inner beauty of the heart. "Charm is deceptive, and beauty does not last; but a woman [or man] who fears the Lord will be greatly praised" (Proverbs 31:30). God continues in 1 Peter 3:3–4, telling us "don't be concerned about the outward beauty of fancy hairstyles, expensive jewelry, or beautiful clothes. You should clothe yourselves instead with the beauty that comes from within, the unfading beauty of a gentle and quiet spirit, which is so precious to God."

Encouragement

Think about the people you know who you consider beautiful. I would be willing to bet that your perception of their outward beauty actually has a lot more to do with their inward beauty. For example, have you ever met someone and just thought "wow, they are stunning" and then after getting to know them more you no longer find them attractive? Or flip that. I'm sure you've met someone in your life who initially you wouldn't have categorized as good looking, only to get to know them and have your entire view change as if you're seeing them through different eyes. True beauty is from within. A person with a beautiful heart will never be ugly.

Self-Study

How did this lie start? *Was it told to you or did you tell it to yourself? Was there a specific moment you started to believe this lie?*

____

____

____

____

____

____

____

____

____

How has this lie affected you? *Has this lie led to certain choices? Has this lie held you back from opportunities or joy?*

____

____

____

____

Make a list of everything you like about yourself. *For example: kind, compassionate, pretty eyes.*

How would your life change if you believed the truth instead of this lie?

Pick a memory verse to repeat to yourself whenever this lie pops into your head and write it here.

LIE:
I will never succeed.

TRUTH:
Success is not measured by your bank account or job title; it is measured by your obedience and love for God.

"Commit your actions to the Lord, and your plans will succeed."
– Proverbs 16:3

"That is why I tell you not to worry about everyday life—whether you have enough food and drink, or enough clothes to wear. Isn't life more than food, and your body more than clothing? Look at the birds. They don't plant or harvest or store food in barns, for your heavenly Father feeds them. And aren't you far more valuable to him than they are?"
– Matthew 6:25–26

Most often people equate success to money. In our minds anyone with money must live a happy and fulfilled life with no worries. It is entirely possible however to have money and a failing marriage or a strained relationship with your children, to be lonely, to hate your job or be in debt. Money does not guarantee success, joy or contentment.

Our world's standards of success are built on fading glory. No matter how much money you make, your status, how many people know your name or how many fancy possessions you own, none of them go with you beyond the grave. On the other side of our short earthly lives lies eternity. I do not say that as fearmongering, I say it because it is the truth, and you deserve to hear it. You get to choose your eternity and it has nothing to do with what the world deems as successful. "And what do you benefit if you gain the whole world but lose your own soul? Is anything worth more than your soul?" (Matthew 16:26).

That is not to say people who are rich in this life will not get into heaven. God does not say that money itself is bad, he says that the love of money is bad (1 Timothy 6:10). Putting aside the love of money, the vanity of status, and setting your eyes and work toward the Lord are how you will find true success. "Work willingly at whatever you do, as though you were working for the Lord rather than for people. Remember that the Lord will give you an inheritance as your reward and that the Master you are serving is Christ" (Colossians 3:23–24). Whatever your circumstance, if you are giving your days to the Lord you are succeeding.

Encouragement

Just like we do not invite everyone into our depths, we do not always get to know the deep and vulnerable parts of the lives of those around us. Do not compare yourself to the story you have made up about the "perfect" person with their "perfectly successful" life standing next to you. We all have problems, every single one of us is an absolute mess, that is why we need God so much. Even in your mess, you are worth more than precious jewels in the sight of your heavenly Father. Shifting your focus to be in a relationship with God is a success that will cause your dreams to grow and flourish.

Self-Study

How did this lie start? *Was it told to you or did you tell it to yourself? Was there a specific moment you started to believe this lie?*

___

___

___

___

___

___

___

___

___

How has this lie affected you? *Has this lie led to certain choices? Has this lie held you back from opportunities or joy?*

Where would you like to see yourself in five years? What can you actively do to start pursuing your goals?

How would your life change if you believed the truth instead of this lie?

____

____

____

____

____

____

____

____

____

Pick a memory verse to repeat to yourself whenever this lie pops into your head and write it here.

____

____

____

____

____

____

____

____

LIE:
I have no gifts or purpose.

TRUTH:
God gives each of us a gift and a purpose.

"God has given each of you a gift from his great variety of spiritual gifts. Use them well to serve one another. Do you have the gift of speaking? Then speak as though God himself were speaking through you. Do you have the gift of helping others? Do it with all the strength and energy that God supplies. Then everything you do will bring glory to God through Jesus Christ. All glory and power to him forever and ever! Amen."
– 1 Peter 4:10–11

"But to each one is given the manifestation of the Spirit for the common good. For to one is given the word of wisdom through the Spirit and to another the word of knowledge according to the same Spirit; to another faith by the same Spirit, and to another gifts of healing by the one Spirit, and to another the effecting of miracles, and to another prophecy, and to another the distinguishing of spirits, to another various kinds of tongues, and to another the interpretation of tongues. But one and the same Spirit works all these things, distributing to each one individually just as He wills."
– 1 Corinthians 12:7–11 (NASB)

"In his grace, God has given us different gifts for doing certain things well. So if God has given you the ability to prophesy, speak out with as much faith as God has given you. If your gift is serving others, serve them well. If you are a teacher, teach well. If your gift is to encourage others, be encouraging. If it is giving, give generously. If God has given you leadership ability, take the responsibility seriously. And if you have a gift for showing kindness to others, do it gladly."
– Romans 12:6-8

"'For I know the plans that I have for you,' declares the LORD, 'plans for welfare and not for calamity to give you a future and a hope.'"
– Jeremiah 29:11 (NASB)

Everyone has a purpose, and you can find yours by identifying the gifts and passions that God has given you. How do you figure out what your spiritual gifts are? You start by identifying what constitutes a spiritual gift. Romans lists seven spiritual gifts as prophesy, serving, teaching, encouragement, giving, leadership, and kindness. First Corinthians adds eight new gifts being, wisdom, knowledge, faith, healing, miracles, discernment, tongues, and interpretation. However, spiritual gifts are not confined to the above list. God hands out spiritual gifts as necessary to fulfill needs in the church and in the world. God knows what he is doing, and he has laid these things on you because they work together for your purpose. "And we know that God causes everything to work together for the good of those who love God and are called according to his purpose for them" (Romans 8:28). Often, we feel pressured to have our life figured out and know our purpose by a young age. When we look at the Bible, though, we see that God does not follow that timeline. There is not an age cap on fulfilling your purpose. Furthermore, when we think of purpose many of us jump to careers—the big question of "what will I do with my life?" Your purpose is so much more than a career, though. God can use your career to benefit your purpose, but your purpose does not end with your job title. Do not let the weight of figuring out your purpose cripple you or stop you from moving forward. God will reveal your purpose to you when the time comes. "You can make many plans, but the Lord's purpose will prevail" (Proverbs 19:21).

Encouragement

If you are unsure what gifts God has given you start by praying that God reveal your gifts to you. It's also helpful to create a list of things that you are good at, or that come easily to you. If you are still at a loss, there are spiritual gift assessments you can take. Many churches offer these tests to help members navigate where to serve, or you can search online for free spiritual gifts tests. Once you identify your giftings, you can begin to research ways to hone your specific gifts.

Self-Study

How did this lie start? *Was it told to you or did you tell it to yourself? Was there a specific moment you started to believe this lie?*

How has this lie affected you? *Has this lie led to certain choices? Has this lie held you back from opportunities or joy?*

How would your life change if you believed the truth instead of this lie?

____

____

____

____

____

____

____

____

Pick a memory verse to repeat to yourself whenever this lie pops into your head and write it here.

____

____

____

____

____

____

____

____

LIE:
I will be happy when I have ________.

TRUTH:
The world may offer temporary happiness, but true lasting joy only comes from knowing your worth and identity in God.

"Don't love money; be satisfied with what you have. For God has said, 'I will never fail you. I will never abandon you.'"
– Hebrews 13:5

"Then he said, 'Beware! Guard against every kind of greed. Life is not measured by how much you own.'"
– Luke 12:15

"Then you will experience God's peace, which exceeds anything we can understand. His peace will guard your hearts and minds as you live in Christ Jesus."
– Philippians 4:7

There is no product you can buy or status you can acquire that will grant you permanent happiness. The problem with believing happiness lies in having more is that when you finally get what you thought you wanted there is always more to have. So instead of being happy you just fill in the blank with the next belonging or position. It is a loop mentality that leaves you constantly longing for bigger and better than what you have.

The world will leave you wanting, but with Jesus you can find a steadfast joy that goes beyond your circumstance. "Not that I was ever in need, for I have learned how to be content with whatever I have. I know how to live on almost nothing or with everything. I have learned the secret of living in every situation, whether it is with a full stomach or empty, with plenty or little. For I can do everything through Christ, who gives me strength" (Philippians 4:11–13).

Encouragement

The world is never going to satisfy the void that Jesus came to fill. What you are lacking is not money, possessions, or status; there is a need that is not being addressed. I encourage you to put deep thought into the self-study of this lie so that you can pinpoint where the feelings of wanting more are coming from. From there you can begin healing and rooting yourself in the love of Jesus where you will find true contentment.

Self-Study

How did this lie start? *Was it told to you or did you tell it to yourself? Was there a specific moment you started to believe this lie?*

How has this lie affected you? *Has this lie led to certain choices? Has this lie held you back from opportunities or joy?*

What void are you trying to fill? *Are you constantly buying the newest electronics to prove you have status? Are you always buying new clothes because you do not feel you are pretty enough or gifting yourself lavishly to feel loved?*

How would your life change if you believed the truth instead of this lie?

Pick a memory verse to repeat to yourself whenever this lie pops into your head and write it here.

LIE:
I can only find joy through drinking/drugs/sex.

TRUTH:
You find distraction in the world; you find peace and healing through Jesus.

"I am overwhelmed with joy in the Lord my God! For he has dressed me with the clothing of salvation and draped me in a robe of righteousness. I am like a bridegroom dressed for his wedding or a bride with her jewels."
– Isaiah 61:10

"When I discovered your words, I devoured them. They are my joy and my heart's delight, for I bear your name, O Lord God of Heaven's Armies."
– Jeremiah 15:16

"You love him even though you have never seen him. Though you do not see him now, you trust him; and you rejoice with a glorious, inexpressible joy. The reward for trusting him will be the salvation of your souls."
– 1 Peter 1:8-9

There is a distinction to be made between what feels good in the moment and true joy. Drinking may dull your pain in the moment, drugs may give you a high or help you forget in the moment, sex may bring pleasure in the moment but none of these things will bring you lasting joy. True joy is a fruit of the spirit given to us by God when the Holy Spirit enters our bodies during salvation. "But the Holy Spirit produces this kind of fruit in our lives: love, joy, peace, patience, kindness, goodness, faithfulness, gentleness, and self-control. There is no law against these things" (Galatians 5:22–23).

Joy is not something that can be faked, because fake joy does not endure the storm. But our God is able to grant us a joy that is steadfast through any trial. "We can rejoice, too, when we run into problems and trials, for we know that they help us develop endurance. And endurance develops strength of character, and character strengthens our confident hope of salvation. And this hope will not lead to disappointment. For we know how dearly God loves us, because he has given us the Holy Spirit to fill our hearts with his love" (Romans 5:3–5). This God-given, lasting joy cannot be found in the world or its distractions; it is achieved only by having faith and trust in the Lord. "I pray that God, the source of hope, will fill you completely with joy and peace because you trust in him. Then you will overflow with confident hope through the power of the Holy Spirit" (Romans 15:13).

Encouragement

Life can be very hard and very messy, causing us to turn to unhealthy habits in an attempt to deal with our pain. Before we know it, we are trapped in a cycle we feel is unbreakable. Thankfully though our God is a chain breaker! Life is so much more than seeking out small moments of escape. If you are struggling with addiction of any kind, I urge you to seek the help of a counselor or support group. You can find contact numbers and websites of applicable resources in the back of the book.

Self-Study

How did this lie start? *Was it told to you or did you tell it to yourself? Was there a specific moment you started to believe this lie?*

How has this lie affected you? *Has this lie led to certain choices? Has this lie held you back from opportunities or joy?*

How would your life change if you believed the truth instead of this lie?

Pick a memory verse to repeat to yourself whenever this lie pops into your head and write it here.

LIE:
I do not need to forgive people who have hurt me.

TRUTH:
Forgiveness is necessary for both peace and healing.

"Make allowance for each other's faults, and forgive anyone who offends you. Remember, the Lord forgave you, so you must forgive others."
– *Colossians 3:13*

"If you forgive those who sin against you, your heavenly Father will forgive you. But if you refuse to forgive others, your Father will not forgive your sins."
– *Matthew 6:14–15*

"God blesses those who are merciful, for they will be shown mercy."
– Matthew 5:7

"Do not judge others, and you will not be judged. Do not condemn others, or it will all come back against you. Forgive others, and you will be forgiven. Give, and you will receive. Your gift will return to you in full pressed down, shaken together to make room for more, running over, and poured into your lap. The amount you give will determine the amount you get back."
– *Luke 6:37–38*

There is a myth that forgiveness is to be granted for the person who did the wrongdoing, only after they have apologized or in some way made amends. The sad truth, though, is that the person who was in the wrong may not value your forgiveness. They may not believe they were in the wrong or, unfortunately, they may not care that they were. But that is okay! Because your forgiveness is not for them, it is for you. It is for you so that chains may be broken, it is for you so that wounds may heal, it is for you so that bitterness does not fester into hate. But what if they do not deserve it?! Neither did you. Neither did I. We have all done things that do not warrant God's forgiveness, yet when asked it was given to us and in turn, he asks that we grant it to others.

Encouragement

Sometimes forgiveness comes instantly, however, more often it is an ongoing process where you daily have to choose to pursue forgiveness while your heart continues to heal. Over time the choice becomes easier, but give yourself grace in the journey. Know that forgiving someone does not mean that you are in any way diminishing the effect that person's words or actions had on you. It does not mean you are minimizing the situation or opening a door for it to reoccur. You may forgive someone and still set safety boundaries for them in the future. Society tells us to hate those who hurt us, but God shows us that only grace brings healing transformation. For more information on setting safe boundaries, visit the resources page in the back of the book.

Self-Study

How did this lie start? *Was it told to you or did you tell it to yourself? Was there a specific moment you started to believe this lie?*

____

____

____

____

____

____

____

____

How has this lie affected you? *Has this lie led to certain choices? Has this lie held you back from opportunities or joy?*

____

Who in your life have you been unable or unwilling to forgive?

When you are ready start praying that God will open your heart to forgiving the people on this list so that you may fully heal.

How would your life change if you believed the truth instead of this lie?

____

____

____

____

____

____

____

____

Pick a memory verse to repeat to yourself whenever this lie pops into your head and write it here.

____

____

____

____

____

____

____

____

LIE:
It is okay for me to hate people who deserve it.

TRUTH:
Hatred will harden and corrupt your heart.

"But I say, love your enemies! Pray for those who persecute you! In that way, you will be acting as true children of your Father in heaven. For he gives his sunlight to both the evil and the good, and he sends rain on the just and the unjust alike."
– Matthew 5:44–45

"Bless those who persecute you. Don't curse them; pray that God will bless them."
– Romans 12:14

"Don't rejoice when your enemies fall; don't be happy when they stumble."
– Proverbs 24:17

"Bless those who curse you. Pray for those who hurt you."
– Luke 6:28

God made us with love, he sent his son to save us through his love and he forgives us out of love. God understands our hearts and what holding on to hatred does to our souls. There are a million reasons why one person would hate another. And the flesh in me wants to tell you so many of those reasons are sound. But the spirit-filled side bites my tongue because though the world shouts that we should hate, the quiet truth is that we do not have too.

Hate is a prison, it takes our time, it consumes our mind, and it drains us entirely. So why would we ever choose to hate when forgiveness is an option? Do not tether yourself to your trauma, do not give hurtful people any more of your time. Choose to love yourself enough to move past hate and to flourish.

Encouragement

There is a place for anger, there are even instances of Jesus showing righteous anger in the Bible (Matthew 21:12). While there is a place and purpose for anger, there is no place for hate. No matter how valid your anger is, hatred is wasteful. You have the choice to refocus your mind to heal, grow, and give your pain a purpose.

Self-Study

How did this lie start? *Was it told to you or did you tell it to yourself? Was there a specific moment you started to believe this lie?*

____

____

____

____

____

____

____

____

How has this lie affected you? *Has this lie led to certain choices? Has this lie held you back from opportunities or joy?*

____

____

____

____

____

How would your life change if you believed the truth instead of this lie?

Has there ever been someone in your life you have wronged who chose to love and forgive you instead of hate? How did it make you feel?

Pick a memory verse to repeat to yourself whenever this lie pops into your head and write it here.

LIE:
Judging others is harmless.

TRUTH:
Only God has the right to judge us.

"Get rid of all bitterness, rage, anger, harsh words, and slander, as well as all types of evil behavior. Instead, be kind to each other, tenderhearted, forgiving one another, just as God through Christ has forgiven you."
– *Ephesians 4:31*

"Do not judge others, and you will not be judged. For you will be treated as you treat others. The standard you use in judging is the standard by which you will be judged."
– *Matthew 7:1–2*

"Do not judge others, and you will not be judged. Do not condemn others, or it will all come back against you. Forgive others, and you will be forgiven."
– *Luke 6:37*

A lot of judgement comes from us trying to convince ourselves that the way others sin is worse than the way we sin. "And why worry about a speck in your friend's eye when you have a log in your own? How can you think of saying to your friend, 'Let me help you get rid of that speck in your eye,' when you cannot see past the log in your own eye? Hypocrite! First get rid of the log in your own eye; then you will see well enough to deal with the speck in your friend's eye" (Matthew 7:3–5). Often, we judge others for being different from ourselves or choosing differently than we do as a defense mechanism. As if their choices are a direct attack on ours. No matter where your judgement is coming from—defensiveness, jealousy, or the best of intentions—it is not your place. "God alone, who gave the law, is the Judge. He alone has the power to save or to destroy. So what right do you have to judge your neighbor" (James 4:12)?

Moreover, God clearly instructs us on how to help hold accountable fellow followers. "Dear brothers and sisters, if another believer is overcome by some sin, you who are godly should gently and humbly help that person back onto the right path. And be careful not to fall into the same temptation yourself. Share each other's burdens, and in this way obey the law of Christ" (Galatians 6:1–2). I want to focus on two specific takeaways from these verses. The first, is that this applies to believers. You will never win a soul to Christ by beating someone over the head with judgement. You cannot hold someone who does not know God to his standards. Instead, you should be focusing on sharing his love and the good news of Jesus. "In the same way, let your good deeds shine out for all to see, so that everyone will praise your heavenly Father" (Matthew 5:16). The second is that when you realize a believer is sinning, you do not judge them, gossip, or punish them; you gently and humbly help them. There is far too much judgment in this world and far too little grace.

Encouragement

I pray that no guilt falls on you after reading this, but that you may repent of any harmful judgmental thoughts or words that you have placed on others. Once we know better, it becomes our duty to do better. Do not dwell on the wrong doing of your past but instead look forward to all the opportunities you have to do better. Do not allow judging others to become a distraction for not working on your own flaws. Every one of us is a work in progress. Use your time and effort for your own betterment instead of the destruction of others.

Self-Study

How did this lie start? *Was it told to you or did you tell it to yourself? Was there a specific moment you started to believe this lie?*

____

____

____

____

How have you felt judged in your life?

How have you judged others in your life?

How has this lie affected you? *Has this lie led to certain choices? Has this lie held you back from opportunities or joy?*

How would your life change if you believed the truth instead of this lie?

Pick a memory verse to repeat to yourself whenever this lie pops into your head and write it here.

Breastplate of Righteousness

LOVE

Depending on your upbringing, culture, and society there are numerous lies and contradictions surrounding what love is and what it should look like. Often how we view love is shaped at a young age by the relationships we witness around us. What we deem as normal and come to expect in relationships is formed by how those around us choose to show us and others love. With so many varying experiences and opinions on love it is best to go to the source (the Bible) for the true definition.

> "Love is patient and kind. Love is not jealous or boastful or proud or rude. It does not demand its own way. It is not irritable, and it keeps no record of being wronged. It does not rejoice about injustice but rejoices whenever the truth wins out. Love never gives up, never loses faith, is always hopeful, and endures through every circumstance." (1 Corinthians 13:4–8)

My hope is that by dissecting the lies in this chapter you realize how deeply God loves you. Not only does he love you fully, but he also wants you to love yourselves and others as fully as he loves you. I pray that identifying the lies surrounding love and focusing on the truth positively impacts how you give and receive love in the future.

LIE:
I am not worth loving.

TRUTH:
Your worth is so great that Jesus died for you.

"What is the price of five sparrows—two copper coins? Yet God does not forget a single one of them. And the very hairs on your head are all numbered. So don't be afraid; you are more valuable to God than a whole flock of sparrows."
– Luke 12:6–7

"For this is how God loved the world: He gave his one and only Son, so that everyone who believes in him will not perish but have eternal life."
– John 3:16

If other people cannot see your worth then that is a problem with them, not you. However, if you cannot see your own worth then we have some work to do. Generally, when we find ourselves questioning our worth it is because we are looking at ourselves through the tinted glasses of society and the lies others have spewed into our minds. The truth, though, is that society does not decide your worth, your parents do not decide your worth, your exes, your friends, and even you do not decide your worth. Your worth is decided by God. Let that sink in. The lie that you are not worth loving is a feeling you have, but the fact that you are worth loving because God created you and deeply loves you is truth. It can not be disputed.

If you are unsure as to how much God loves and values you, turn to Romans 5:8 for the answer: "God showed his great love for us by sending Christ to die for us while we were still sinners." What this means is that even at our lowest—in all of our brokenness, in the addiction, the crimes, sexual sin, harmful actions, hate-filled words—in the midst of all of it, God sees worth in you. God loves you.

Encouragement

Loneliness can contribute to the feeling of worthlessness. I want to challenge you to step out of your comfort zone and into a community. For you that could mean joining a small group at church or finding a hobby group. God built us to live in community with each other, lifting each other up and carrying each other's burdens. "Let us think of ways to motivate one another to acts of love and good works. And let us not neglect our meeting together, as some people do, but encourage one another, especially now that the day of his return is drawing near" (Hebrews 10: 24–25).

Self-Study

How did this lie start? *Was it told to you or did you tell it to yourself? Was there a specific moment you started to believe this lie?*

____

____

____

____

____

____

____

____

How has this lie affected you? *Has this lie led to certain choices? Has this lie held you back from opportunities or joy?*

____

____

____

Create a list of good things about yourself. *This could include compliments from others, or things you like or are proud about.*

Add to this list as often as you can and reflect on it when you feel unworthy.

How would your life change if you believed the truth instead of this lie?

Pick a memory verse to repeat to yourself whenever this lie pops into your head and write it here.

LIE:
I will never be loved.

TRUTH:
You have been known and loved fully since the moment God created you in the womb.

"And I am convinced that nothing can ever separate us from God's love. Neither death nor life, neither angels nor demons, neither our fears for today nor our worries about tomorrow—not even the powers of hell can separate us from God's love. No power in the sky above or in the earth below—indeed, nothing in all creation will ever be able to separate us from the love of God that is revealed in Christ Jesus our Lord."
– Romans 8:38–39

"We love each other because he loved us first."
– 1 John 4:19

"Give thanks to the God of heaven. His faithful love endures forever."
– Psalm 136:26

Personally, I believe this is one of the worst lies the devil lays on us. Out of the 1,189 chapters in the Bible, not one of them ever contradicts God's love for us. First John 3:1 tells us to "See how very much our Father loves us, for he calls us his children, and that is what we are!" At times, our actions may anger God, if we choose to reject him it hurts him, but through it all he loves us. Furthermore, throughout the Bible we are perpetually called to love each other. "Most important of all, continue to show deep love for each other, for love covers a multitude of sins" (1 Peter 4:8). "So now I am giving you a new commandment: Love each other. Just as I have loved you, you should love each other" (John 13:34). "And do everything with love" (1 Corinthians 16:14). If you are in an environment or relationship where someone is speaking the lie over you that you will never be loved, know that there are advocates available to you through community centers and some churches.

Encouragement

In Jesus's name I pray that this lie the devil has placed in your heart, that you will never be loved, is thrown out of your mind and cast into the sea. I pray that in every moment moving forward you are cloaked in knowing that you are completely and irrevocably loved by God, our Father. May all of your future steps be made in the confidence of your worth in him.

Self-Study

How did this lie start? *Was it told to you or did you tell it to yourself? Was there a specific moment you started to believe this lie?*

____

____

____

____

____

____

____

____

How has this lie affected you? *Has this lie led to certain choices? Has this lie held you back from opportunities or joy?*

____

____

____

____

____

How would your life change if you believed the truth instead of this lie?

Pick a memory verse to repeat to yourself whenever this lie pops into your head and write it here.

LIE:
I have to earn God's love.

TRUTH:
God's love is given, not earned.

"God saved you by his grace when you believed. And you can't take credit for this; it is a gift from God."
– Ephesians 2:8

"And I am convinced that nothing can ever separate us from God's love. Neither death nor life, neither angels nor demons, neither our fears for today nor our worries about tomorrow—not even the powers of hell can separate us from God's love. No power in the sky above or in the earth below—indeed, nothing in all creation will ever be able to separate us from the love of God that is revealed in Christ Jesus our Lord."
– Romans 8:38–39

This is such a deeply rooted lie that it has even penetrated many religious sects as doctrine. I understand the logic of doing good deeds to earn a reward. We are programmed to believe that good acts merit good things and bad acts merit bad things. In the confines of our world that sometimes holds true. However, in the unbounded greatness of God, our actions do not dictate his love. I think one of the main issues with this lie is that people have a hard time separating love and salvation. There is no requirement for God's love. He gives it to you freely, whether you want it or not. If you are worried that God does not love you because you are not a Christian, I suggest reading the second lie *God only cares about Christians* in the first chapter.

Again, God's love is freely given, no action required, although salvation requires faith. "If you openly declare that Jesus is Lord and believe in your heart that God raised him from the dead, you will be saved" (Romans 10:9). It does not say you have to be perfect or donate all your belongings to charity or never watch a movie rated higher than PG, it says you have to believe. It is your faith that grants you salvation, not your actions. You may not take credit for what God gifts you as a believer.

Encouragement

God can and will forgive every sin that you repent of and will love you regardless of your past, present, or future. At any moment in time, you have the opportunity to choose a relationship with Jesus. In entering that covenant, Jesus's blood pays for every sin. Your good deeds will not earn you God's love, because you cannot earn what you already have, they will add to your rewards in heaven, though. "But I, the Lord, search all hearts and examine secret motives. I give all people their due rewards, according to what their actions deserve" (Jeremiah 17:10).

Self-Study

How did this lie start? *Was it told to you or did you tell it to yourself? Was there a specific moment you started to believe this lie?*

____

____

____

____

____

____

____

____

How has this lie affected you? *Has this lie led to certain choices? Has this lie held you back from opportunities or joy?*

____

____

____

What are the things you do currently or have done in the past to try and earn God's love?

How would your life change if you believed the truth instead of this lie?

Pick a memory verse to repeat to yourself whenever this lie pops into your head and write it here.

LIE:
Love is pain.

TRUTH:
Love is work, it can be tough, but abuse, torment and destruction are not of love.

"Such love has no fear, because perfect love expels all fear. If we are afraid, it is for fear of punishment, and this shows that we have not fully experienced his perfect love."
– *1 John 4:18*

"Love means doing what God has commanded us, and he has commanded us to love one another, just as you heard from the beginning."
– *2 John 1:6*

To break down this lie, it is important to understand the difference between the ever-changing roller coaster of emotions the world labels as "love" and the pure everlasting love that God grants us and commands us to grant to others. Worldly love can cause pain and heartbreak, but the love of our God will never fail us. "Give thanks to the LORD, for he is good! *His faithful love endures forever*" (Psalm 136:1). God lays out very clearly in 1 Corinthians 13:4–7 what love actually is: "Love is patient and kind. Love is not jealous or boastful or proud or rude. It does not demand its own way. It is not irritable, and it keeps no record of being wronged. It does not rejoice about injustice but rejoices whenever the truth wins out. Love never gives up, never loses faith, is always hopeful, and endures through every circumstance." This is the pure, pain-free love that God has for us and that he wants us to have with others. Unfortunately, humans come with flaws, baggage, and expectations that taint how we give and receive love. Love in its true form is without pain, however love filtered through human emotion is a forever growing process that can be messy.

Encouragement

If you are currently in an abusive relationship or marriage please seek help through a domestic violence victim advocate, therapist, or church counselor. You can find helpful contact information on our resources page in the back of the book. There is no shame, guilt, or sin in leaving an unchanging, unrepentant, abusive partner. Your life and safety matter.

Self-Study

How did this lie start? *Was it told to you or did you tell it to yourself? Was there a specific moment you started to believe this lie?*

____

____

____

____

____

____

____

____

How has this lie affected you? *Has this lie led to certain choices? Has this lie held you back from opportunities or joy?*

____

____

____

____

____

How would your life change if you believed the truth instead of this lie?

Pick a memory verse to repeat to yourself whenever this lie pops into your head and write it here.

LIE:
Love should be effortless.

TRUTH:
Love and relationships require hard work.

"If you love only those who love you, what reward is there for that?
Even corrupt tax collectors do that much."
– *Matthew 5:46*

"If you love only those who love you, why should you get credit for that?
Even sinners love those who love them!"
– *Luke 6:32*

"Hatred stirs up quarrels, but love makes up for all offenses."
– *Proverbs 10:12*

Love is a choice. If it were not a choice God would not have called us to love others as he loved us (John 15:12). If loving everyone came naturally God would not have to command us to do it, and if we were not capable of choosing to love people God would not have instructed it. We are told in 1 John 3:18, "Little children, let us not love in word or talk but in deed and in truth." God is telling us not to rely on words alone but to use our actions. The dictionary defines the word "deed" as "an intentional act" (Cambridge English Dictionary). Meaning that God is calling us to go beyond going through the motions and to intentionally and consciously put in the effort to choose love. There will be seasons when choosing love is easy, but there will also be seasons where love will be the hardest choice you have ever made.

Encouragement

When you struggle to choose love over anger, resentment, bitterness, fairness, or judgement I urge you to step back and think of all the times God chose to love you in your brokenness. Do not get me wrong, loving someone does not require putting yourself at risk or enabling others. What it does require is responding with a clear head and kindness.

Self-Study

How did this lie start? *Was it told to you or did you tell it to yourself? Was there a specific moment you started to believe this lie?*

How has this lie affected you? *Has this lie led to certain choices? Has this lie held you back from opportunities or joy?*

How would your life change if you believed the truth instead of this lie?

Pick a memory verse to repeat to yourself whenever this lie pops into your head and write it here.

LIE:
I am not a virgin so practicing abstinence now would be pointless.

TRUTH:
You are never at a point where you cannot decide to turn and live a life following Christ.

"Therefore, if anyone is in Christ, the new creation has come: The old has gone, the new is here!"
– 2 Corinthians 5:17

"By no means! We are those who have died to sin; how can we live in it any longer?"
– Romans 6:2

"You were taught, with regard to your former way of life, to put off your old self, which is being corrupted by its deceitful desires; to be made new in the attitude of your minds; and to put on the new self, created to be like God in true righteousness and holiness."
– Ephesians 4:22–24

"God's will is for you to be holy, so stay away from all sexual sin. Then each of you will control his own body and live in holiness and honor."
– 1 Thessalonians 4:3–4

"Flee from sexual immorality. All other sins a person commits are outside the body, but whoever sins sexually, sins against their own body."
– 1 Corinthians 6:18

God invented sex. And it may astound you to know that God wants you to have great sex, in the confines of marriage. As with all of God's commandments, abstinence till marriage is not God's way of being a buzzkill or trying to control us. God's commandments are to keep us physically, mentally, and emotionally safe while providing the best possible life.

The reason we are so greatly warned about sexual sin is because of the profound impact sex has on our mind, body, and spirit. What feels good in the moment can have devastating consequences in the long run. Please do not allow the fact that you are not a virgin to lead you down a destructive path that does not honor your body or your worth. One of the most joyous things about our Lord, is that he forgives and renews. If you lost your virginity or are having sex of your own free will, know that "if we confess our sins, he is faithful and just and will forgive us our sins and purify us from all unrighteousness" (1 John 1:9). If having sex was not your choice, please read the *I was raped so sex does not matter anymore* lie in chapter three.

Encouragement

Having a past does not take away your right to honor your body in the present. One of the most beautiful things about being human is that we constantly get to grow and change for the better. Do not let your own self talk or the talk of others hold you back from everything God has for you today.

Self-Study

How did this lie start? *Was it told to you or did you tell it to yourself? Was there a specific moment you started to believe this lie?*

___

___

___

___

___

___

___

___

___

___

How has this lie affected you? *Has this lie led to certain choices? Has this lie held you back from opportunities or joy?*

How would your life change if you believed the truth instead of this lie?

Pick a memory verse to repeat to yourself whenever this lie pops into your head and write it here.

Shoes of Peace

HOPELESSNESS & LONELINESS

Throughout the Bible there are countless references to the importance of advisors and living in community. As early as Genesis 2 we are told that we are not meant to walk alone, "Then the LORD GOD SAID, 'IT IS NOT GOOD FOR THE MAN TO BE ALONE. I WILL MAKE A HELPER WHO IS JUST RIGHT FOR HIM" (Genesis 2:18). God's reasoning for wanting us to have community goes beyond our emotional wellbeing. He knows that the devil will use isolation to wear down our mental health and self-worth. "A person standing alone can be attacked and defeated, but two can stand back-to-back and conquer. Three are even better, for a triple-braided cord is not easily broken" (Ecclesiastes 4:12). We are not intended to be alone; it is the devil that works so diligently to separate us from others so that we may become easier pray. Community is important, talking about your thoughts and feelings are important. "As iron sharpens iron, so a friend sharpens a friend" (Proverbs 27:17). Culture has tried to convince us that it is a weakness to need others, but the Bible shines light on the truth that we are to share each other's burdens and lift each other up.

Akin to loneliness, the devil wants to keep you in a mindset of hopelessness because he knows that hope is powerful. Hope is a seed that grows and multiplies. "Let us hold tightly without wavering to the hope we affirm, for God can be trusted to keep his promise" (Hebrews 10:23). Without hope we are numb and stagnant. With hope we open up to the opportunity to dream and flourish. "I pray that your hearts will be flooded with light so that you can understand the confident hope he has given to those he called—his holy people who are his rich and glorious inheritance" (Ephesians 1:18). If you are struggling with hopelessness, be assured that it is safe to hope in the Lord because he does not lie and he does not fail. "But blessed are those who trust in the Lord and have made the Lord their hope and confidence" (Jeremiah 17:7). Guard your heart and mind from the devil and dive into the Bible to find all the strength and hope God has to offer. "You are my refuge and my shield; your word is my source of hope" (Psalm 119:114).

LIE:
Things will never be better.

TRUTH:
There is always light to be found in the darkness.

"But those who trust in the LORD will find new strength. They will soar high on wings like eagles. They will run and not grow weary. They will walk and not faint."
– *Isaiah 40:31*

"He led them from the darkness and deepest gloom; he snapped their chains."
– *Psalms 107:14*

"Yet what we suffer now is nothing compared to the glory he will reveal to us later."
– *Romans 8:18*

I do not think anyone would argue that life is easy. The good news though is that our lives are made up of seasons, some good and some bad. Some seasons are longer than others, but there is no season of your life that will last forever. I understand the heaviness and hopelessness of truly believing that the darkness you are sitting in is a lifetime sentence. I understand the crippling feeling of each minute dragging out for what seems like days. Thankfully though, I also understand the release of coming out of that darkness and taking a full breath in the light. I'm pleading with you to be present for this moment when it happens for you, and it will happen for you. True transformational change comes through having a relationship with Jesus. Faith is powerful. Mark 11:23 says "Truly I tell you, if anyone says to this mountain, 'Go, throw yourself into the sea,' and does not doubt in their heart but believes that what they say will happen, it will be done for them." Do not settle for the bad. God has granted you the capability to change your circumstances. Whether that looks like staying in the circumstance and changing it from within or walking away from a toxic environment, God has equipped you with the strength needed.

Encouragement

You have the ability to speak good things into your life. "It is the same with my word. I send it out, and it always produces fruit. It will accomplish all I want it to, and it will prosper everywhere I send it" (Isaiah 55:11). Proverbs 18:21 tells us that the power of life and death is in our tongue. Make sure you are speaking life over yourself.

Self-Study

How did this lie start? *Was it told to you or did you tell it to yourself? Was there a specific moment you started to believe this lie?*

____

____

____

____

____

____

____

____

How has this lie affected you? *Has this lie led to certain choices? Has this lie held you back from opportunities or joy?*

____

____

____

____

____

Think of things you can start doing for yourself that will brighten your day. *This could be beginning daily affirmations, listening to your favorite song, anything that will add a bit of happiness to your day.*

How would your life change if you believed the truth instead of this lie?

Pick a memory verse to repeat to yourself whenever this lie pops into your head and write it here.

LIE:
Evil will always win.

TRUTH:
Evil does not prevail.

"But the wicked will be blinded. They will have no escape.
Their only hope is death."
– Job 11:20

"For the wicked will be destroyed, but those who trust in the LORD
will possess the land. Soon the wicked will disappear.
Though you look for them, they will be gone."
– Psalm 37:9–10

"For the Lord your God is going with you! He will fight for you against
your enemies, and he will give you victory!"
– Deuteronomy 20:4

"Put on all of God's armor so that you will be able to stand firm
against all strategies of the devil."
– Ephesians 6:11

"I have told you all this so that you may have peace in me. Here on
earth you will have many trials and sorrows. But take heart,
because I have overcome the world."
– John 16:33

If you are unfamiliar with the Bible you may not realize that though there is a lot of mystery in our stories, we know the end. God defeats the devil; evil does not win! In the book of Revelations, John has a vision from God in which he tells us "the devil who had deceived them was thrown into the lake of fire and sulfur where the beast and the false prophet were, and they will be tormented day and night forever and ever" (Revelations 20:10). Often in the midst of a storm it can seem like we are fighting a losing battle, but in the war we are victorious. In the moments where it feels like good is failing and you are questioning if doing the right thing matters, you can turn to 1 Peter 3:14 for the answer; "But even if you suffer for doing what is right, God will reward you for it. So don't worry or be afraid of their threats." Another key thing to recognize when going up against evil is that we are not truly fighting each other, but rather combating the sins, brokenness and manipulations of the devil. "For we are not fighting against flesh-and-blood enemies, but against evil rulers and authorities of the unseen world, against mighty powers in this dark world, and against evil spirits in the heavenly places" (Ephesians 6:12). If you are struggling with how to better fight your battles, I highly suggest you read Ephesians 6 to learn more about putting on the full armor of God for protection and strength.

Encouragement

I want to encourage you with this advice from Mr. Fred Rogers, "When I was a boy and I would see scary things in the news, my mother would say to me, 'Look for the helpers. You will always find people who are helping.'" I challenge you to not only look for the helpers but to become one for others.

Self-Study

How did this lie start? *Was it told to you or did you tell it to yourself? Was there a specific moment you started to believe this lie?*

____

____

____

____

____

____

____

How has this lie affected you? *Has this lie led to certain choices? Has this lie held you back from opportunities or joy?*

How would your life change if you believed the truth instead of this lie?

Pick a memory verse to repeat to yourself whenever this lie pops into your head and write it here.

LIE:
God has forgotten me.

TRUTH:
God knows all of his creations by name, you are never forgotten.

"Never! Can a mother forget her nursing child? Can she feel no love for the child she has borne? But even if that were possible, I would not forget you!"
– *Isaiah 49:15*

"And be sure of this: I am with you always, even to the end of the age."
– *Matthew 28:20*

"What is the price of five sparrows—two copper coins? Yet God does not forget a single one of them. And the very hairs on your head are all numbered. So don't be afraid; you are more valuable to God than a whole flock of sparrows."
– *Luke 12:6–7*

"Do not be afraid or discouraged, for the LORD will personally go ahead of you. He will be with you; he will neither fail you nor abandon you."
– *Deuteronomy 31:8*

Let me assure you, you are not forgotten. God knows you; he sees you and he loves you deeply. If you do not know God, I promise he knows you. God created you lovingly in your mother's womb. He knows every fiber of your being and he wants to have a relationship with you.

If you are a follower of Christ, you have full access to the voice of God. "My sheep listen to my voice; I know them, and they follow me. I give them eternal life, and they will never perish. No one can snatch them away from me" (John 10:27-28). In times where God seems quiet it can be easy to become fearful that we have been overlooked. Just because God is silent, though, it does not mean he is absent. He is present with you always, offering you his comfort, strength and directing your path.

Encouragement

The world can make us feel insignificant and tossed aside. That is why it is so important to root your worth in who God says you are. And God says that you are fearfully and wonderfully made (Psalms 139:14). In the Hebrew text the word fearfully translates to mean with great reverence, heart-felt interest, and respect. You have been created and you are loved by the one true God and that makes you unforgettable.

Self-Study

How did this lie start? *Was it told to you or did you tell it to yourself? Was there a specific moment you started to believe this lie?*

____

____

____

____

____

____

____

____

How has this lie affected you? *Has this lie led to certain choices? Has this lie held you back from opportunities or joy?*

____

____

____

____

How would your life change if you believed the truth instead of this lie?

Pick a memory verse to repeat to yourself whenever this lie pops into your head and write it here.

LIE:
I have nothing to be thankful for.

TRUTH:
There is always something to be thankful for if you open your eyes to it.

"Always be joyful."
– 1 Thessalonians 5:16

"We serve God whether people honor us or despise us, whether they slander us or praise us. We are honest, but they call us impostors. We are ignored, even though we are well known. We live close to death, but we are still alive. We have been beaten, but we have not been killed. Our hearts ache, but we always have joy. We are poor, but we give spiritual riches to others. We own nothing, and yet we have everything."
– 2 Corinthians 6:8–10

A thankful person will always find a reason to give thanks, on the flip side an ungrateful person will always find something they lack. Being thankful is a mindset. For instance, if you are a thankful person and have a car, you are thankful for it. If you do not have a car you are thankful for your bike, if you do not have a bike you are thankful for your legs, and if you are wheelchair bound you are thankful for the wheels. If you are ungrateful however, it does not matter if you have a car, because you want a better car or a private jet. When you start to truly dissect what you are thankful for, or rather the lack of your thankfulness, you will find where you place your priorities and worth.

The root of being unthankful is in misplaced priorities and false idols. If we are not careful, money, romance, and status can quickly become things we idolize over God. "Wherever your treasure is, there the desires of your heart will also be" (Matthew 6:21). It is important to recognize what you treasure, if you are placing your treasures above God, and to adjust as needed.

Encouragement

I encourage you to take some quiet time to yourself and start a list of things to be thankful for. Begin to write down everything and anything you are thankful for, no matter how small it seems or how much you take it for granted. For example, maybe you are thankful for coffee, electricity, taking a walk, or a smile from a stranger. After writing your initial list, begin to actively seek out things and moments to add to your list daily. Let this become a regular reminder to yourself that you not only have things to be thankful for, but that you are abundantly blessed!

Self-Study

How did this lie start? *Was it told to you or did you tell it to yourself? Was there a specific moment you started to believe this lie?*

____

____

____

____

____

____

____

____

How has this lie affected you? *Has this lie led to certain choices? Has this lie held you back from opportunities or joy?*

____

____

____

How would your life change if you believed the truth instead of this lie?

Start your list of things you are thankful for below.

Pick a memory verse to repeat to yourself whenever this lie pops into your head and write it here.

LIE:
I will always live in fear.

TRUTH:
God calls us to step out beyond our fear.

"So be strong and courageous! Do not be afraid and do not panic before them. For the LORD your God will personally go ahead of you. He will neither fail you nor abandon you."
– *Deuteronomy 31:6*

"When doubts filled my mind, your comfort gave me renewed hope and cheer."
– *Psalm 94:19*

"But even if you suffer for doing what is right, God will reward you for it. So don't worry or be afraid of their threats."
– *1 Peter 3:14*

Fear and worry play an important role in our lives. Fear places certain necessary boundaries, such as keeping us from running into traffic or diving into shark infested waters. Too often, though, we allow fear and worry to take over our mind, control our thoughts, and decide our every action. Instead of acting as a helpful survival tool, fear traps us in a cage that keeps us from living to our full potential. If we are not careful, what starts as a small worry can quickly avalanche, taking down everything in its wake. Matthew 6:34 warns us, "don't worry about tomorrow, for tomorrow will bring its own worries. Today's trouble is enough for today."

God does not expect us never to worry, but he does want our faith in him to outweigh our fear. The closer you grow to God, the further you will be from fear. Not only will growing closer to God distance you from fear, it will allow you greater access to the power he gives you. "Look, I have given you authority over all the power of the enemy, and you can walk among snakes and scorpions and crush them. Nothing will injure you" (Luke 10:19). Never forget that you walk in authority, that you are capable, and you are powerful.

Encouragement

This does not mean that your fears are not valid. They are. You may have experienced trauma in the past, have PTSD, or currently be in the midst of an unsafe situation. Whatever your circumstance, I encourage you to speak to someone who will hear out your fears and help you navigate them. If you are in an abusive relationship, please reach out to a domestic violence victim advocate for help with safety planning. You do not have to live in fear. "For God has not given us a spirit of fear and timidity, but of power, love, and self-discipline" (2 Timothy 1:7).

Self-Study

How did this lie start? *Was it told to you or did you tell it to yourself? Was there a specific moment you started to believe this lie?*

____

____

____

____

____

____

____

____

____

How has this lie affected you? *Has this lie led to certain choices? Has this lie held you back from opportunities or joy?*

____

____

How would your life change if you believed the truth instead of this lie?

Pick a memory verse to repeat to yourself whenever this lie pops into your head and write it here.

LIE:
I will never have joy.

TRUTH:
Joy is a choice that you have open access to.

"I have told you these things so that you will be filled with my joy.
Yes, your joy will overflow!"
– John 15:11

"So you have sorrow now, but I will see you again; then you will rejoice,
and no one can rob you of that joy."
– John 16:22

The world would like us to believe that happiness is free, love is easy, and you should not have to work at something if it is meant to be. The problem with this worldview is that it is full of lies that leave us constantly tossing aside the good and longing for more. I will never forget sitting in our pre-marital counselor's office and her telling us that my now husband's happiness was not my responsibility, and that my happiness was not his, to which I immediately decided we needed to find a new counselor. Turns out, though, she was right. My joy is no one's responsibility but my own. I do not know about you, but for me that was an awfully hard truth to swallow. That does not change it from being the truth. Every morning we wake up and decide how to take on the day. Every time someone speaks to or of us, we get to choose which of their words to cling to and which to lay down. Choosing joy on a day filled with sunshine is easy but choosing joy in the storm requires strength. "The Lord is my strength and shield. I trust him with all my heart. He helps me, and my heart is filled with joy. I burst out in songs of thanksgiving" (Psalm 28:7). Choosing joy takes dedication and strength, it's intentional. Know, though, that you do not have to find this strength alone, God will cover whatever you lack.

Encouragement

"I pray that God, the source of hope, will fill you completely with joy and peace because you trust in him. Then you will overflow with confident hope through the power of the Holy Spirit" (Romans 15:13).

Self-Study

How did this lie start? *Was it told to you or did you tell it to yourself? Was there a specific moment you started to believe this lie?*

How has this lie affected you? *Has this lie led to certain choices? Has this lie held you back from opportunities or joy?*

How would your life change if you believed the truth instead of this lie?

Pick a memory verse to repeat to yourself whenever this lie pops into your head and write it here.

LIE:
I will never be understood.

TRUTH:
God knows you fully, even better than you know yourself.

"You made all the delicate, inner parts of my body and knit me together in my mother's womb. Thank you for making me so wonderfully complex! Your workmanship is marvelous—how well I know it. You watched me as I was being formed in utter seclusion, as I was woven together in the dark of the womb. You saw me before I was born. Every day of my life was recorded in your book. Every moment was laid out before a single day had passed."
– Psalm 139:13–16

"O Lord, you have examined my heart and know everything about me."
– Psalm 139:1

"And the Father who knows all hearts knows what the Spirit is saying, for the Spirit pleads for us believers in harmony with God's own will."
– Romans 8:27

God created you. He knows and fully understands every part of you. We all long to be understood and accepted, to be loved even in our worst moments. Sometimes though, in fear, we board our hearts and build walls, terrified that if we are honest and real no one will love or even like us when it is actually the opposite. The more we break down our barriers and allow others to see we are broken, the greater the opportunity for connection becomes. That little voice telling you no one will understand you is Satan desperately trying to keep you hidden in the dark because he knows the minute you start sharing, being real, and stepping into the light is when he loses his grip on you. The devil thrives in the dark; every step you take towards openness and light scares him. You have the choice to let the darkness keep its hold or to step into the sun. If you never give people the chance to understand and connect with you, they never will.

Encouragement

One of the reasons so many of us feel misunderstood is because we think no one else feels the way we do. I guarantee though there is not an emotion you have experienced that someone, somewhere on Earth, has not felt too. Our feelings, thoughts, experiences, and traumas only separate us if we allow them to.

Self-Study

How did this lie start? *Was it told to you or did you tell it to yourself? Was there a specific moment you started to believe this lie?*

____

____

____

____

____

____

____

____

How has this lie affected you? *Has this lie led to certain choices? Has this lie held you back from opportunities or joy?*

____

____

____

____

____

How would your life change if you believed the truth instead of this lie?

Pick a memory verse to repeat to yourself whenever this lie pops into your head and write it here.

LIE:
I will always be alone.

TRUTH:
The Holy Spirit lives within believers and because of this we are never alone.

"Even when I walk through the darkest valley, I will not be afraid,
for you are close beside me. Your rod and your staff
protect and comfort me."
– *Psalm 23:4*

"Do not be afraid or discouraged, for the LORD will personally go ahead of you. He will be with you; he will neither fail you nor abandon you."
– *Deuteronomy 31:8*

"God is our refuge and strength, always ready to help in times of trouble."
– *Psalm 46:1*

"'For I hold you by your right hand— I, the Lord your God. And I say to you, 'Don't be afraid. I am here to help you.'"
– *Isaiah 41:13*

I always find it so interesting when I hear someone say, "they found God" as if he were hiding. This statement could not be further from the truth. Though there will be times in your life where God is silent, he is never gone. God loved us so much that he sent his son to die on a cross so that we may be forgiven and filled with the Holy Spirit. If you are a saved believer, just as you can never be apart from yourself, you can never be apart from God because the Holy Spirit lives inside you.

There are times where we are capable of feeling alone even in a crowded room. This feeling of distance can affect any relationship. And it is important to remember that our walk with God is a relationship. Just like any other relationship, you have to put work into it to feel connected. If you are not feeling that God is present with you, dive into his word so that you may grow closer to him.

This does not mean that you are alone if you are not saved. God loves you, and he is beside you waiting for you to accept him. God does not hide or turn his back on us. He waits and longs to welcome all of us into his arms with love.

Encouragement

God created us to live in community with one another. "Share each other's burdens, and in this way obey the law of Christ" (Galatians 6:2). Maybe you have tried to engage in small groups before and it did not work out. Do not let that dissuade you from trying a different group. Keep searching until you find your place, because I promise there is one for you.

Self-Study

How did this lie start? *Was it told to you or did you tell it to yourself? Was there a specific moment you started to believe this lie?*

____

____

____

____

____

____

____

____

____

How has this lie affected you? *Has this lie led to certain choices? Has this lie held you back from opportunities or joy?*

____

How would your life change if you believed the truth instead of this lie?

Pick a memory verse to repeat to yourself whenever this lie pops into your head and write it here.

LIE:
I will always be broken.

TRUTH:
No one is perfect, but God can and will make us whole and bring beauty from ashes.

"He heals the brokenhearted and bandages their wounds"
– Psalm 147:3

"Each time he said, 'My grace is all you need. My power works best in weakness.' So now I am glad to boast about my weaknesses, so that the power of Christ can work through me."
– 2 Corinthians 12:9

So, you think you are broken? The truth is we all are. The only perfect person was Jesus, meaning that the rest of us fall somewhere on the "broken but holding it together" to "complete train wreck" spectrum at all times. The good news is that God wants your brokenness! Where we break his light can shine through. Nowhere in the Bible does it state that you will not have a bad day, experience loss, or make a mistake. All of these things make us human. We all break in different ways, but those cracks make us compassionate, relatable, and they are opportunities for us to learn and grow in our walk with God.

When we talk about being broken it often comes with a very negative stigma attached, but this does not have to be the case. Breaking is not a weakness it is a transition process. I pray that you may begin to see the beauty in your broken pieces and how breaking can allow for us to mold into beautiful new forms.

Encouragement

Bettering yourself is a life-long process. Everyone has room for growth. If you will stop running from your brokenness, lean in, and lay it at his feet you will be astounded by the things he can do. Our God creates beauty from ashes!

Self-Study

How did this lie start? *Was it told to you or did you tell it to yourself? Was there a specific moment you started to believe this lie?*

How has this lie affected you? *Has this lie led to certain choices? Has this lie held you back from opportunities or joy?*

Make a list of moments in your life when you have felt strong.

Reflect on this list and know that being broken does not equate to weakness.

How would your life change if you believed the truth instead of this lie?

Pick a memory verse to repeat to yourself whenever this lie pops into your head and write it here.

Put on God's Full Armor

God has equipped each of us with the necessary weapons to fight the devil's manipulations. Use what he has put in your arsenal to protect your body, heart, mind, and soul.

The Whole Armor of God

> "A final word: Be strong in the Lord and in his mighty power. Put on all of God's armor so that you will be able to stand firm against all strategies of the devil. For we are not fighting against flesh-and-blood enemies, but against evil rulers and authorities of the unseen world, against mighty powers in this dark world, and against evil spirits in the heavenly places.
>
> Therefore, put on every piece of God's armor so you will be able to resist the enemy in the time of evil. Then after the battle you will still be standing firm. Stand your ground, putting on the belt of truth and the body armor of God's righteousness. For shoes, put on the peace that comes from the Good News so that you will be fully prepared. In addition to all of these, hold up the shield of faith to stop the fiery arrows of the devil. Put on salvation as your helmet, and take the sword of the Spirit, which is the word of God.
>
> Pray in the Spirit at all times and on every occasion. Stay alert and be persistent in your prayers for all believers everywhere."
>
> – Ephesians 6:10–18

Salvation Prayer

"If you openly declare that Jesus is Lord and believe in your heart that God raised him from the dead, you will be saved."
– *Romans 10:9*

The Bible does not give us specific words for the salvation prayer, but if you are ready to accept Jesus and start a relationship with him, I would be honored to help guide you in prayer. Remember that without faith these are just words, but with faith, they are a life-changing signing of your passport to heaven.

"Father God, I am broken, I have sinned,
and I have been far from you.
Please forgive me.
Come into my heart,
guide my steps,
transform me through your Holy Spirit.
I want to know and walk in your light.
Thank you for loving me and for sending your son Jesus
to die on a cross as payment for my sins so that I may
spend eternity close to you.
In Jesus's name, Amen!"

Congratulations!!! The angels are celebrating your salvation in heaven right now! "In the same way, there is joy in the presence of God's angels when even one sinner repents" (Luke 15:10).

The next step: After salvation comes public baptism. Please reach out to a pastor near you to share your wonderful news so that they may help guide you through this next important process.

Self-harm Alternatives & Coping Skills

If you are struggling with self-harm, please know you are not alone and that there are several resources available to help and comfort you. If you are unable or uncomfortable reaching out to family or friends, most churches have on-staff counselors or referral counselors they can get you in contact with. I know the thought of asking for help can be paralyzing, it takes immense courage to speak out loud the pain hiding in your head and heart, but I promise you God will be there every moment. There are so many people waiting to love and support you if you will just reach out and let them in.

Below is a list of coping skills and alternatives you may use when the urge to inflict self-harm hits you. This list is meant for you to have easy access to safe alternatives in your time of need, it is meant to work in conjunction with and not as a substitute to counseling or support group therapy.

"Don't you realize that your body is the temple of the Holy Spirit, who lives in you and was given to you by God?"
– 1 Corinthians 6:19–20

Minimize Harm

- Place a thick elastic or rubber band around your wrist and snap it
- Draw on yourself instead of cutting
- Hit pillows or cushions

Shock Your Senses

- Hold ice cubes or run them along where you want to cut yourself
- Take a cold bath or shower

Let it Out

- Scream into a pillow
- Vent in a journal
- Play music and sing loudly

Distractions

- Pray
- Go for a walk
- Exercise
- Draw
- Color
- Read
- Get crafty
- Meditate

Resources

Sexual Assault

- **National Sexual Assault Hotline US**
    - Phone: 1-800-656-4673
    - Chat online: www.rainn.org
- **National Human Trafficking Hotline US**
    - Phone: 1-888-373-7888 TTY 711
    - Text 233733
    - Chat online: www.humantraffickinghotline.org
- **Rape and Sexual Assault Support Centre UK**
    - Women and girls aged 13+ call 0808 802 9999

Domestic Violence

- **National Domestic Violence Hotline US**
    - 1-800-799-7233 or TTY 1-800-787-3224
    - Online chat: www.thehotline.org
- **Love Is - National Teen Dating Abuse Hotline US**
    - People aged 13–26 call 1-866-331-9474
    - Text: 22522
    - Online chat: www.loveisrespect.org
- **Refuge National Domestic Abuse Helpline UK**
    - Phone: 0808 2000 247
    - Online chat: www.nationaldahelpline.org.uk

Self-harm and Suicide

- **National Suicide Prevention Lifeline US**
    - 1-800-273-8255

- Online chat: www.suicidepreventionlifeline.org

- **Crisis Text Line US**
  - US: Text 741741
  - CA: Text 741741
  - UK: Text 85258
  - Ireland: Text 50808
  - Online chat: www.crisistextline.org

- **Crisis Services Canada**
  - Phone: 1-833-456-4566
  - Text 45645
  - Online chat: www.crisisservicescanada.ca/en

- **Campaign Against Living Miserably UK**
  - Phone: 0800 58 58 58
  - Webchat: www.thecalmzone.net

Addiction and Mental Health

- **Substance Abuse and Mental Health Services National Helpline US**
  - Phone: 1-800-662-4357

- **National Alliance on Mental Illness US**
  - 1-800-950-6264
  - Text NAMI to 741-741
  - Online chat: www.nami.org

- **Canadian Centre on Substance Abuse and Addiction**
  - For local resources within Canada, visit www.ccsa.ca/addictions-treatment-helplines-canada

- **Alcoholics Anonymous US and Canada**
  - A.A is an international fellowship of men and women who have had a drinking problem. To find a meeting near you, visit www.aa.org/pages/en_US/find-aa-resources

- **Alcoholics Anonymous UK**
  - To locate a meeting near you, visit www.alcoholics-anonymous.org.uk

- **Narcotics Anonymous Worldwide**
    - NA is a nonprofit fellowship of men and women for whom drugs had become a major problem. To locate a meeting near you, visit www.na.org/meetingsearch

Support

- **SupportLine UK**
    - The Helpline is primarily a preventative service and aims to support people before they reach the point of crisis. It is particularly aimed at those who are socially isolated, vulnerable, at risk groups and victims of any form of abuse.
    - Phone: 01708 765200
- **Samaritans England, Whales Ireland, and Scotland**
    - Available for anyone who is struggling to cope and needs someone to listen without judgement or pressure.
    - Phone: 116 123.
    - Welsh language 0808 164 0123
    - Online chat: www.samaritans.org
- **Ending Violence Association of Canada**
    - Shelters, sexual assault, domestic violence, crisis support, and other resources near you. Visit www.endingviolencecanada.org/getting-help/
- **Celebrate Recovery**
    - Celebrate Recovery is a Christ-centered, 12-step recovery program for anyone struggling with hurt, pain, or addiction of any kind. To locate a meeting with in the US, visit www.celebraterecovery.com
    - To find international meetings, visit www.celebraterecovery.com/cr-international
- **Al-Anon US**
    - AlAnon is a mutual support program for people whose lives have been affected by someone else's drinking. You can find in-person meetings near you or join telephone meetings at

www.al-anon.org/al-anon-meetings

- **Al-Anon UK and Eire**
    - Phone: 0800 0086 8
    - To find a meeting near you, visit
    www.al-anonuk.org.uk/find-a-meeting

Recommended Reading

1. Cloud, H., & Townsend, J. S. (1992). *Boundaries: When to say yes, when to say no to take control of your life.* Zondervan.
2. Townsend, J. S. (2011). *Beyond boundaries: learning to trust again in relationships.* Zondervan.
3. TerKeurst , L. (2016). *Uninvited: Living Loved When You Feel Less Than, Left Out, and Lonely.* Nelson Books.

About the Author

Billie-Jewel Sexton is the founder of Bridge the Gap, a ministry that works to make the church a safe, inviting, and accepting place for survivors of domestic and sexual abuse. As a survivor herself, she works to help others through awareness, education, and sharing the healing power of Jesus. Billie-Jewel has an interdisciplinary bachelor's degree with a focus in social and behavioral sciences from Liberty University. She also worked at the Young Women's Christian Association (YWCA) as a domestic violence victim advocate before leaving to be home with her son and pursue God's calling on her heart to ministry. Billie-Jewel, her husband, Sean, and their children make their home in Tennessee.

Made in the USA
Columbia, SC
21 December 2023